Uncertainty impacts us all, but our perception of it is often fragmented and ill-defined. Melanie Kreye brings clarity to the concept and provides a much-needed synthesis of diverse research findings. Using topical examples, she has written an accessible guide to this fascinating field, highlighting the pitfalls we should avoid if we are to survive and prosper in an uncertain world.

Paul Goodwin, University of Bath, UK

This book offers a new way of explaining how uncertainty can be managed from the lens of the soft side. The focus on people (part 1) and organizations (part 2) is a substantial step forward from uncertainty management. The book gives the definition of uncertainty and provides various examples of how people and organizations deal with decisions under uncertainty. Good read.

Prof. Dr. Marly Monteiro de Carvalho –
University of São Paulo.

Uncertainty and Behaviour

Uncertainty affects us in our every-day lives, and in a wide range of situations. How do individuals and indeed organisations respond to uncertainty and how does it impact their decision-making and actions? Based on the latest developments in academic research, the author offers solid advice on how to manage uncertainty in every-day life, bringing a new perspective to these issues and extrapolating this to offer implications for an organisational and managerial context. The author brings this emerging area of research to a wider audience by:

- Tying together insights from various academic fields including psychology, engineering, business and management.
- Creating a framework for usefully applying the research concepts in every-day life.
- Extrapolating insights from the psychology of individual decision makers to the organisational context and managerial decision-making.
- Creating highly applicable and impactful recommendations for how managers and organisations can understand and manage uncertainty.

The book is divided into two main parts. Part I deals with the behaviour of individuals facing uncertainty and includes accessible explanations and examples of every-day applications, while Part II deals with behaviour in organisations facing uncertainty to explore how, for example, (mis)-perceptions and decision-making biases impact managerial life. This is a must read for both managers and those who are seeking to better understand their own behaviour and management approach.

Melanie E. Kreye is an Assistant Professor at the Technical University of Denmark (DTU) in the Department of Management Engineering. Her research focuses on uncertainty in business and management, particularly its impact on organisational decision-making and on service operations. She has worked and published on this issue with organisations in Europe and worldwide.

Uncertainty and Behaviour

Perceptions, Decisions and Actions in Business

MELANIE E. KREYE
Technical University of Denmark, Lyngby, Denmark

Routledge
Taylor & Francis Group

LONDON AND NEW YORK

First published 2016
by Routledge

2 Park Square, Milton Park, Abingdon, Oxfordshire OX14 4RN
52 Vanderbilt Avenue, New York, NY 10017

Routledge is an imprint of the Taylor & Francis Group, an informa business

First issued in paperback 2020

British Library Cataloguing in Publication Data
A catalogue record for this book is available from the British Library

Library of Congress Cataloging-in-Publication Data
Names: Kreye, Melanie E., author.
Title: Uncertainty and behaviour : perceptions, decisions and actions
    in business / by Melanie E. Kreye.
Description: Farnham, Surrey, UK ; Burlington, VT : Gower, [2016] |
    Includes bibliographical references and index.
Identifiers: LCCN 2015037274 | ISBN 9781472482419 (hardback) |
    ISBN 9781472482426 (ebook) | ISBN 9781472482433 (epub)
Subjects: LCSH: Decision making. | Uncertainty. | Problem solving. |
    Management.
Classification: LCC HD30.23 .K75 2016 | DDC 658.4/0301—dc23
LC record available at http://lccn.loc.gov/2015037274

ISBN: 978-1-4724-8241-9 (hbk)
ISBN: 978-0-367-66971-3 (pbk)

Typeset in Constantia
by Apex CoVantage, LLC

Contents

List of Figures and Tables

Figures

Tables

CHAPTER 1

Introduction

Uncertainty has been a phenomenon featuring in many academic investigations, and is at the core of many theories explaining behaviours and observations in business. Almost a century of research has highlighted the importance of uncertainty in various areas in our lives. Uncertainty impacts decision making, enables us to develop trust with friends and family and establish stable relationships, and impacts our experience of fairness at work and the interpretation and meaning of language and words. Uncertainty is related to all experimental measurements, surrounding any prediction into the future and thus the development of economies in general. Andrzej Koźmiński stated in 2015 that "Uncertainty is the price we have to pay for freedom" and thus put it at the core of the challenges in most, if not all, parts of our lives.

Uncertainty triggered my interest from the very start of my research activity, although in the beginning this manifested itself more as annoyance and frustration. As a Ph.D. student focusing on a topic that integrated mechanical engineering, management and decision making, my first task was to review the literature in these fields to integrate different insights and findings. I found it difficult, to say the least, to make head or tail of these writings. The understandings of uncertainty between the different fields were ill-aligned and even contradictory. However, the more I read about it, the more this issue stimulated my interest.

Different Fields – Different Viewpoints

Other scholars agree with this assessment and repeatedly highlight the large scope for interesting debates. John Mackey, a researcher in the field of music, wrote "Uncertainty should continue to be seen as an exciting challenge" and Sasha Grishin, a researcher in the history of art, agrees: "uncertainty [is] a liberating force". New and exciting research is being published on uncertainty on a regular basis, shedding light on the concept from different viewpoints and in different empirical settings. Doing a keyword search on academic databases such as Scopus shows the increasing role uncertainty plays in the academic literature over recent decades. This includes papers in conferences, academic journals and books. The number of publications[1] has increased almost 100-fold over a period of 40 years from 1,839 in the 1960s to 162,637 in the 2000s (see also Figure 1.1). Thus the chances are that a scholar is racking their brains about the issue right now, while you are reading this book (it might even be me).

So, What Is Uncertainty, and What Is It Not?

My intrinsic understanding of what uncertainty is (before I had read any academic articles about it) relates it to a general lack of knowledge. If I don't know (enough) about a problem or area, I feel uncertain about it. When I am not sure about the leaving or arrival times of a train, I am uncertain as to when I will be at a friend's house – and I might express this uncertainty by saying "around 5 o'clock" or "5ish". Similarly, in organisations, the number of sales in 5 or 10 years' time is uncertain.

However, in many languages other than English, this understanding is not that clear. In fact, many of these languages have multiple words for the concept of uncertainty. In German, for example, uncertainty can be *Unsicherheit*, *Ungewissheit* and *Unbestimmtheit*, each meaning different things. *Unsicherheit* literally translates as a situation of not being sure. This means that there can

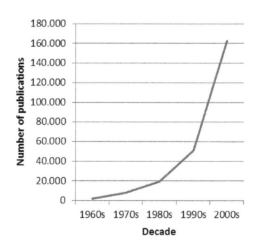

FIGURE 1.1 ACADEMIC PUBLICATIONS ON UNCERTAINTY

---

1   Mentioning "uncertainty" in the title, keywords or abstract.

be some variation as to the true value. I might arrive between quarter to 5 and quarter-past at my friend's house, for example. But at least we know a ballpark figure, just with some possible variation around it. In contrast, *Ungewissheit* refers to knowledge that we cannot derive logically. This term would apply to the future sales of a company. Innovations and changes in the market and economy might derive any prediction about future sales wrong. Third, *Unbestimmtheit* typically applies to measurements. Heisenberg's uncertainty principle translates to German as the *Unbestimmheitsrelation*[2]. Similar variations and differentiations can be found in other languages.[3]

WHAT DO THE EXPERTS HAVE TO SAY?

The variation is reflected in the academic literature.[4] Similar to the meaning arising from the different translations of uncertainty into German, there are also three different understandings in the academic literature. The first set of definitions describes uncertainty as a completely controllable phenomenon and the task of research is to find suitable approaches to model and simulate this uncertainty. This is similar to the German word *Unsicherheit* because there is a general understanding about the situation or problem which gives us a ballpark figure, but not a definite and clear answer. Researchers falling into this category typically seek to describe uncertainty probabilistically through repetitive observations and trials. The basic assumption is that uncertainty needs to be controlled and that modelling it offers suitable means for identifying most likely outcomes as well as best-case and worst case scenarios.

Take for example the water level of a river such as the Elbe in Germany. Say you needed to estimate this water level because you want to set up a business of tourist boats and the depth of the water impacts whether you can operate your ships. The average water level of the Elbe is about 1.98 m but is highly variable from season to season. In extreme cases these fluctuations can give water levels of down to 0.3 m (measured during the low water of 1954) and up to 9.4 (during the flood in 2002).[5] Despite the large variability and

---

2   The principle is sometimes also referred to as *Unschärfe* relation which literally translated to fuzziness principle.

3   In Danish, for example, there are two words: usikkerhed and *ubestemthed*.

4   Although many papers (often as many as 50 per cent) do not even provide a definition, which is rather careless.

5   Admittedly, these are extreme events that occur rarely but when they do they have extreme impacts. In fact, these two events placed the area around the Elbe and whole cities and states in emergency situations for months.

complexity of influences, it is (theoretically) possible to build a model that considers factors such as temperature, precipitation and the river discharge. The model can show the Elbe's water levels.[6] This makes it possible to prepare and plan for the uncertainty and take action accordingly.

The second set of definitions describes uncertainty as a phenomenon that cannot be controlled but can be influenced. As such, uncertainty is the *absence of information* or the difference between the information someone has and the information they need. This gap can be reduced. If I am uncertain as to the actual length of the river Elbe, I can look it up. I can reduce my uncertainty by collecting further information. This definition also suggests that uncertainty is something negative and unwanted. When I am uncertain, I feel panicked and insecure and I want to get away from this situation and become certain. I want to acquire enough knowledge that I will not come into situations of being uncertain – or at least not often.

The third set of definitions sees uncertainty as a completely uncontrollable phenomenon. We can model uncertainty and simulate outcomes, but the resulting predictions are fundamentally flawed. There is some unknown variable – luck, destiny or something else – that changes plans and predictions. I can measure uncertainty but I cannot influence or control it. As such, some situations are inherently more uncertain than others.

For example, consider the difference between an orchestra player and a jazz musician. Both are very skilled musicians and yet they use their skills in very different ways, and one way to look at this is through the lens of uncertainty. Uncertainty can give the freedom to create and be creative. An orchestra player would probably perceive little uncertainty as to the music they will be playing because the piece would be agreed with the rest of the orchestra and the rhythm and speed would be determined by the conductor. In contrast, jazz includes improvisations, a sequence of music that is created spontaneously and is thus uncertain, yet the result is often very fascinating and much loved by the audience.

HOW DOES THIS FIT TOGETHER?

Uncertainty can mean quite different things to different people – and this difference in definition can lead to quite different research outcomes. So what definition is applicable in the context of behaviour and organisations? Looking

---

6   Calculating this is quite a complicated process. One example was given by Monica Ionita in her PhD thesis at Bremen University in 2009, entitled "Variability and potential predictability of Elbe river streamflow and their relationship to global teleconnection patterns."

at the definitions a little closer, it seems they are not as incompatible as they first appear. Depicting them as a Venn diagram looks something like Figure 1.2.

Imagine you would like to start a new hobby, something you have never done before – say knitting. You have no experience in it and thus face uncertainty: What needles are you to use? What techniques are there? What can and cannot be knitted? You can reduce that uncertainty by finding information about how best to approach knitting – find tutorial videos online or find a local interest group – or by practicing. The uncertainty is not a completely uncontrollable phenomenon for you because you can try to reduce it. In this example, uncertainty seems to be a reducible phenomenon.

Similarly when an organisation – say a manufacturer of cars – starts to engage a new valve supplier, they face uncertainty. Will the new supplier deliver the requested quality? Will the deliveries be on time? Do they have alternative and self-serving motives? Part of this uncertainty can be reduced. The car manufacturer can look into the supplier's history, contact previous or other existing customers and gather information about the new provider. The uncertainty can be reduced, but only to a point. Some uncertainty will remain in this situation. For example, it will not be possible to completely ascertain the supplier's motives or their future level of cooperation. Again, uncertainty seems to be a reducible phenomenon rather than a completely controllable or completely uncontrollable one.

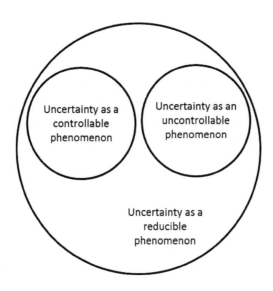

FIGURE 1.2 DEFINITIONS OF UNCERTAINTY

UNCERTAINTY AND RISK

Many of the discussions I have had over the years, and in fact many of the discussions between researchers in this field, evolve around the difference between uncertainty in comparison to risk. There are many other related concepts – ambiguity, complexity, imprecision, inexperience, contradicting opinions and so on – but the comparison between uncertainty and risk is the most frequent and probably also the oldest of the discussions.

So what is the difference between uncertainty and risk? When am I risking something as opposed to ... – what is the verb of uncertainty? The difference can be found exactly in this: the *something*. I risk *something*. I risk my life when I cycle without a helmet, I risk losing money when I gamble, I risk being late to a meeting. I cannot *uncertain*[7] these things. This means in risk there is an impact on something. We can then make our decisions or take appropriate actions depending on the severity of this impact and the frequency with which these risk events happen.

Look for example at the graph in Figure 1.3. I listed some of the risk events in my life. Quite a boring life, you may think, though I would call it a risk-managed life. In any case, in the graph you can see that some risk events in my life have a higher frequency than others. They can also have different levels of impact on my life which vary according to how dependent I am on them. For example, it happens quite regularly that I forget my mobile phone (at home, at work, etc.) and when I do, the impact on my life is relatively low because I can also communicate via other tools. In contrast, if I miss work because I am ill, I find this rather annoying and the impact is quite high. But it also happens quite rarely. You may choose to make a map like this for your own life. If you identify a risk event with a high frequency and a high impact, this is where risk management becomes a crucial tool. In this case, you may want to read one of the many books on risk management or alternatively contact your insurance broker for some help.

In this text I will be looking at uncertainty, and I hope through the course of this book it will become clear why I chose this focus over risk. I can summarise these reasons in two points. First, I find uncertainty a very exciting and interesting research area. Its importance has been highlighted by numerous authors and research fields and reading up on new findings is always fascinating to me. Second, uncertainty has received much less focused research interest. There are numerous books on risk management: a search on Amazon finds

---

7   If we assume this to be a verb. I apologise to anyone who feels offended by this misuse of the English language.

FIGURE 1.3 RISK EVENTS IN MY LIFE

almost 95,000 titles. Uncertainty is a much less explored research area, and this has raised my curiosity and enthusiasm about this topic.

UNCERTAINTY, KNOWLEDGE AND INFORMATION

Uncertainty as I understand it and will explore it in this book is a lack of knowledge – there is something relevant that we do not know, or we do not know it exactly. Thus uncertainty relates directly to existing knowledge – the more knowledge I have about a topic, the less uncertain I am about it. Conversely, the less I know about something, the more uncertain I am. Uncertainty and knowledge are negatively correlated. Figure 1.4 depicts that graphically.

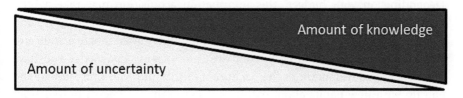

FIGURE 1.4 AMOUNT OF UNCERTAINTY VS AMOUNT OF KNOWLEDGE

Researchers call this the uncertainty cone. It represents different amounts of uncertainty depending on the amount of available knowledge. The uncertainty cone is often depicted over time, which assumes that the longer you work on a topic – knitting, for example – the more knowledge you accumulate and the less uncertain you are. For the purpose of this description, we use Figure 1.4 without time lines. The left-hand corner of the figure shows a situation with a large amount of uncertainty and no knowledge about it. This is referred to as ignorance. Something is not only unknown, but also unknowable. For example, think of the time when the Internet was in its baby shoes – the late 1980s and early 1990s. No one really knew yet what advantages it could bring or what market opportunities it would open up. This was an unknowable future. A similar situation was the advent of television in the 1920s when the technology was being developed and the possibilities and ultimate impacts on our lives were not only unclear but unknowable. We knew nothing about these situations at that time.

In contrast, the right-hand corner of the figure shows a situation with no uncertainty where we have all relevant knowledge. This is a situation of certainty. Everything is clear – or is at least clear enough to make a confident decision. For example, try to make a decision as to whether you cook at home tonight or whether you go to a local restaurant. One consideration is what it would cost to eat out. If you know the restaurant well and you have eaten there before, you can make a pretty good guess about the costs of eating out. The prices vary depending on the dish, but you will be confident enough in making the decision as to whether to go there or eat at home. You face a situation of low uncertainty or high certainty because you have a high level of knowledge about the menu.

We can move along the uncertainty cone by acquiring knowledge. So how do we acquire knowledge? We build knowledge when we acquire new information. Imagine for example that you move to a new city and amongst many other things, you do not know the local restaurants. You do not know about their prices, which restaurant you would prefer and which local dishes you might like. But you can acquire this information by testing the restaurants. Depending on your budget, this information acquisition may take a little longer, but at some point you will know the situation in your new town. You find the relevant information about the restaurants (price range, distance to your house, dishes served etc.), compare it to existing knowledge you have (the other local restaurant or the restaurant in your previous home town) and end up with new habits about eating out. For example, when I moved from the UK to Denmark, I reduced the amount I ate out simply because it is more expensive. I was uncertain about the eating-out situation in Denmark, acquired new information about the situation here – and left some money behind along the way. I moved from high uncertainty to low uncertainty.

UNCERTAINTY AND TIME

This means that the level of uncertainty changes. Uncertainty and time are linked, and this link is a strange one because uncertainty and time are both positively and negatively correlated. On the one hand, uncertainty resolves with time. If I am uncertain about something today, the problem may have solved itself by tomorrow. Bedford and Cooke described this in a chapter of their 2001 book, *What is Uncertainty?*, as "Uncertainty is that which disappears when we become certain". When I decide in the morning whether or not to take an umbrella with me, I am uncertain about the weather during the day. Will it rain? Will it be windy? This uncertainty resolves itself during the day and I may regret my decision when I stand at the bus stop in the pouring rain after deciding not to take the umbrella. Uncertainty and time can be negatively correlated. As time passes, uncertainty can resolve itself.

One the other hand, uncertainty increases with the time span we are looking at. If I had to make the decision on Sunday as to whether to take an umbrella every single day of the coming week, perhaps because I am travelling and will not be home to pick it up during the week, the uncertainty I face increases. For Monday, I may be able to make a relatively confident estimate about the best action but by Friday the weather may have changed significantly.[8] Thus the further we look into the future, the more uncertainty we face. Uncertainty and time span can be positively correlated.

This dichotomy has also entered our behaviour as we respond differently to uncertainty depending on time. People usually prefer an early resolution of uncertainty. If you placed a bid to buy a house, you might be waiting for the phone call that tells you if your offer was accepted. You might even lose sleep until this moment arrives and the uncertainty is resolved. On the other hand, people may also like the eagerness that comes with waiting for the uncertainty to resolve because it gives a period of hopeful anticipation (think back to your childhood when you were waiting for Christmas and the moment when you could open your presents). We can make a similar observation when we watch

---

8   This obviously depends on where you live. In Denmark, for example, the weather in the next half an hour is pure speculation and I have been surprised by unanticipated showers on many occasions.

people gamble – the moment before the roulette ball stops at a certain number and reveals whether the player has won or lost is usually filled with anticipation.

Dealing with Uncertainty

Uncertainty is a key challenge of persons and of organisations. Hugh Courtney and his co-authors argued in their 1997 article in the *Harvard Business Review* that "underestimating uncertainty can lead to strategies that neither defend against the threats nor take advantage of the opportunities that higher levels of uncertainty may provide" (p. 4). In other words, ignoring uncertainty can create problems – sometimes large problems. One often quoted example was the assessment of Kenneth H. Olsen, then the President of the Digital Equipment Corporation. In 1977, he said that "there is no reason for any individual to have a computer in their home". How different the world looks today.

Uncertainty is intrinsic to all our decisions – in our private lives as much as in our professional lives. And yet it is difficult to deal with it – how can you make sure that you make the right choice when you are missing information? When do we go for the safe bet? Kahneman and Tversky wrote in an academic paper that "A comprehensive psychological perspective on uncertainty ... reveals a variety of processes and experiences, ranging from such basic mechanisms as habituation to repeated stimulation in a single neurone, to such complex activities as the evaluation of scientific hypotheses." In other words, people experience the existence of uncertainty very differently. Similarly, people react to decision making under uncertainty very differently. There are models and frameworks to understand the influences of uncertainty on behaviour. The behaviour we show on a personal level also affects our decisions at work. In this book, we will investigate how we make decisions on an individual level when facing uncertainty, and subsequently, what this means for whole organisations.

Aim of this book

This book brings the insights from the latest developments in academic research to the real world and explains how these insights apply to our personal and professional lives. The book is about how people and organisations perceive, decide and act under the influence of uncertainty. We will look at how people respond to uncertainty in different situations and offer insights on how to manage uncertainty in every-day life. The book's objective is to bring this emerging area of research to a wider audience outside of the core academic fields by (1) tying together insights from various fields including psychology, engineering, business and management, and (2) extrapolating insights from the psychology of individual decision makers to the organisational context and managerial decision-making.

Book Structure

This book is divided into two parts. In Part I, we will look at individuals and uncertainty. This is the classic viewpoint of research in this topic and we will look at work from researchers in fields such as psychology, social sciences and behavioural economics. We will answer questions such as: What is it that we do when we face uncertainty? How do we act? And why do we react in these ways?

In Part II, we will look at organisations and their behaviour in the light of uncertainty. This is a more novel perspective on uncertainty and its impact on behaviour. We will investigate whether similarities can be drawn between individual behaviour and organisational behaviour when facing uncertainty. We will answer questions such as: How do organisations act when they face uncertainty? And why do they react in these ways?

PART I
PEOPLE AND UNCERTAINTY

The first part of this book focuses on people and uncertainty. We look at the individual level and the influence that uncertainty has on us and our lives. What do we do when we face uncertainty? How do we decide and how do we act in the face of the unknown? How does it impact the friendships we form, the directions in which we drive our lives and the paths that we leave behind?

We will look at the following five issues:

- Perceiving uncertainty
- Expressing uncertainty
- Accepting uncertainty
- Deciding under uncertainty
- Acting on uncertainty.

CHAPTER 2

Perceiving Uncertainty

Aden was occupied in 1839 by the

a) British?
b) French?

Bile pigments accumulate as a result of a condition known as

a) Gangrene?
b) Jaundice?

What are the correct answers to these two questions? And how high would you put the probability that your answer is correct? Is it a complete guess? Then you would give a probability of 50 per cent. Do you know for certain? Then you would answer 100 per cent. Or is it something in between?

When answering knowledge questions such as the two posed above, we may feel uncertain. Assessing your answer and your own level of uncertainty about its correctness has been a way for researchers to assess the perception of uncertainty. This can be used to judge how accurate our perception is in comparison to the actual uncertainty – which can be measured in the amount of answers you state correctly. And the finding is that these two differ – the uncertainty we perceive is typically different from the uncertainty we actually face.

Uncertainty and Uncertainty Perception

We often perceive uncertainty attached to our level of knowledge in a specific way. Many researchers have used questions such as the two above[1] to assess whether people are accurate in assessing their own level of knowledge and thus

---

1   In fact, these two questions are taken from a study presented by Sarah Lichtenstein and Baruch Fischhoff entitled "Do those who know more also know more about how much they know?"

their level of perceived uncertainty. In particular, the research groups around Baruch Fischhoff, Sarah Lichtenstein and Paul Slovic have contributed to the insights in this area. Their motivation for this research was decision theory in economics. Decision economics aims at predicting decision outcomes based on various assumptions about our behaviour. One of these assumptions is that we perceive situations accurately, exactly how they are. If I am completely uncertain about the answers to the questions above, I would give a probability value of 50 per cent – as it is completely down to luck whether I picked the right answer of the two given choices. In contrast, if I remember I have learned something about the questions, say at school, but I cannot immediately recall what the answer is, I may pick a probability value of 70 per cent. Decision economics states that these probabilities are the true values of uncertainty in these situations and we can thus calculate the optimal decision outcome based on them. It sounds plausible at first sight.

Some psychology researchers were not so convinced by the practical value of this assumption. They argued that we are not able to accurately assess a situation. Imagine you have been on a holiday with someone – your spouse, your friend or your parent. When you come back home you meet with other friends and describe your experience during the holiday – what you have done, what you have seen, what you have eaten. You start explaining particular events and your spouse, friend or parent chips in with anecdotes as you go along. At some point, the conversation may be interrupted when your holiday partner says "No, actually what happened is that ... " This is an example of how we recall experiences differently because we perceive them differently at the time. Chances are that if you had brought a third holiday partner, this person would bring a third viewpoint to the table. We perceive situations differently and in all likelihood neither of us perceives it "correctly" or exactly as it happened.

Lichtenstein and Fischhoff[2] tested this observation in the context of uncertainty. They asked various people general knowledge questions such as those listed at the beginning of this chapter. They then asked these people to assign a probabilistic value of how sure they were that their answers were correct. These probability values spread between 50 per cent – when their answer was a complete guess – and 100 per cent – when they were completely sure their answer was correct. They then measured the proportion of correct answers in dependence on the given probability statements. For example, if one of the study participants stated 50 per cent as a probability value for 10 of their answers, how many of these answers were actually correct? If the 50 per cent statement is accurate, it should be 5 out of the 10 answers. Using this method they were able to compare stated probability values with the proportion of correct answers. And what they found was quite interesting.

They were able to plot the given answers in a graph similar to the one shown in Figure 2.1. The horizontal axis (x-axis) shows the stated probability values by the participants, the vertical axis (y-axis) shows the proportion of correct answers. If economic decision theory is correct, Lichtenstein and Fischhoff would have observed values along the dotted diagonal line – the "should-be curve". However, what they saw in the experiment was slightly different from this. Their observations were more along the lines of the "as-is curve".[3]

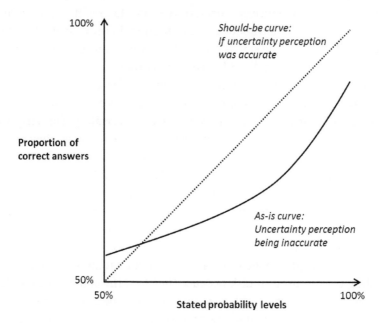

FIGURE 2.1 SHOULD-BE AND AS-IS OF UNCERTAINTY PERCEPTION

---

3   In fact, they did multiple iterations of the study with different subjects and different levels of general knowledge questions, tested the impact of training, experimental set-up and various other factors which meant they observed an "as-if curve" for these different factors. The one presented in Figure 2.1 is an approximation of the overall findings presented in their research papers.

The as-if curve is sometimes above the should-be curve, specifically for low probability values of close to complete luck. This means that if a study participant gave the probability value of 50 per cent to 10 of their answers, they were actually correct 6 times, rather than the 5 times they should have been correct. The main part of the as-is curve, however, is underneath the should-be curve. This reflects study participants that gave a probability value of say 80 per cent to 10 of their answers but were only correct for 7 of them. It seems to be the case that we are better at estimating some probabilities values than others.

The studies by Lichtenstein and Fischhoff show that there is a fundamental difference between a situation and our perception of this situation. In terms of uncertainty we say that a situation may contain extant uncertainty. This can be observed in terms of the proportion of correct answers – the should-be curve. There is also perceived uncertainty – the statement that an individual will say they are uncertain about a given situation. In the described studies this could be observed in the stated probability levels. Thus extant and perceived uncertainties fundamentally differ from each other.

Uncertainty perception impacts many of our decisions and actions. When I feel I don't know enough about an assignment, I will look for relevant information in order to reduce this perceived uncertainty. Similarly, when a company does not have the competencies to complete a task, they may reach out to other companies that do have these competencies. Consider for example a company that manufactures hearing aids and delivers these to customers such as local clinics, consultants or specialist stores. Their marketing department has identified that customers want smaller and lighter devices but the company does not know how to achieve this. One main obstacle is to produce batteries that are smaller than their predecessors and yet powerful enough to support the hearing aid. The manufacturer faces uncertainty regarding this innovation task because they lack the competency to develop this new type of hearing aid in-house. It might be a good idea to involve their battery supplier in this task and work together on producing smaller batteries. The hearing aid manufacturer would be able to manufacture the equipment their customers want and the supplier would be able to develop batteries that are more targeted to their customers' needs (i.e. the hearing aid manufacturer). A win–win situation. The hearing aid manufacturer leaps into action after perceiving uncertainty. Uncertainty perception is core to many organisational and individual decisions, and yet so often we get it wrong.

Uncertainty Perception and Confidence

In the eye of uncertainty, people make decisions with a specific level of confidence. This is a feeling of knowing something. Confidence is something we express when making a statement such as "The chance of rain tomorrow is 30 per cent". The 30 per cent states our level of confidence in that opinion. In this case, the statement is quantitative as it is expressed in a number or percentage. Confidence can be expressed in many ways, including qualitatively. If for example you do not have the necessary computer power to forecast tomorrow's weather but would like to make a statement based on other information you have, you may say "I think it may rain tomorrow". In this case, the "I think" fulfils the same task as the 30 per cent in the statement above but is a qualitative rather than a quantitative expression.

Confidence and uncertainty are directly linked. If the uncertainty is high, the confidence should be low. If I am uncertain, I am less confident, and the less confident my statements should be. For example, if I have seen tomorrow's weather forecast, my statement may be quite confident. I may announce that "It is really unlikely that it will rain tomorrow". In contrast, if I have not seen any substantiated forecast and would have to make up an opinion as I am being asked about it, I may state that "I don't think it will rain tomorrow". Depending on the information I have available at the time, my confidence changes and so accordingly does my statement. Thus confidence seems to be a measurable instrument of people's uncertainty perception.

I KNOW SOMETHING YOU DON'T KNOW

The link between uncertain and confidence has been used in research to identify how people make choices when they are faced with different uncertainty situations. Research about our psychology to test reactions to different situations and influences is typically undertaken with experiments.[4] In experiments, researchers invent a scenario that the study participants have to

---

4   Technically these studies are so-called quasi-experiments, because the study context cannot be 100 per cent controlled as it can in, for example, chemical experiments. When people participate in studies, they may have had a stressful or particularly good day. They may have received praise from a colleague or a telling-off from their spouse. These are all factors that cannot be controlled by researchers which is why a separate name was introduced to account for these factors.

go through. This can be a puzzle they have to solve, a set of questions they have to answer or activities they have to perform.

One of the favourite experiment scenarios in uncertainty research is games, especially where chance is a core element for winning the game. The reasons for this are threefold. First, the probability can be accurately determined which means that the extant uncertainty is known. This is important because it allows the researchers to compare the study participants' perceived uncertainty to the extant uncertainty. For example, if I tell you that with a standard dice I can throw the number 3 in 50 per cent of my throws, you can compare my perceived uncertainty (50 per cent) to the extant uncertainty (17 per cent) and judge that I am overconfident.[5]

The second reason for using games in experimental research is that outcomes can be immediately observed. Based on my statement about throwing the number 3 for 50 per cent of the time, we can test this claim by throwing the dice 20 times and see what happens. This is important for experimental research because the participant is not only told about a fact but can "experience" it. Imagine you participate in such an experiment, where you are asked to roll the dice multiple times and are asked to estimate what number the next throw will be. By observing the throws you make, you can adjust your estimates. You do not need to take the study facilitator's word for it when they say the dice are not manipulated, but you can base any further decisions on your own observations. This makes your reactions more realistic and closer to how you would decide in other uncertain situations.

The third advantage of games is that the extant uncertainty cannot be influenced by the participants. The probability of throwing any one number when rolling dice is one in six; the chances of getting heads when throwing a coin are 50 per cent and the likelihood of winning a lottery is also predetermined by the total amount of available tickets. Thus the rules of the game are set, and what is particularly intriguing is that the participants know the rules and yet often depart from the implications they have. This gives researchers the possibility of making strong inferences based on the observations of their experiments.

In these gambling experiments, participants are typically asked to predict the outcome of their decisions or actions and assign a confidence level to it. For example, Ellen Langer and her co-authors asked students to judge their own ability to predict the outcome of a coin toss. The coin was not manipulated so we can assume that the probability of throwing either heads or tails is

---

5   Let us assume that the dice are "perfect" and hence not manipulated so that one number, such as the 3, shows significantly more often than the expected 1 in 6 (i.e. 17 per cent) of all throws.

50 per cent each. The students have the choice to predict either heads or tails as a throw outcome and the probability of being right is thus also 50 per cent. Hence, the extant uncertainty of the participants' prediction being right – irrespective of whether it is head or tails – is 50 per cent. Yet the researchers made an interesting observation about the perceived uncertainty.

A stunning difference could be observed depending on the success of the first few throws. Naturally, some of the participants were correct in their prediction of the first few throws. The probability states that 50 per cent will be correct in correctly predicting the first throw, 25 per cent (= 0.5*0.5) in predicting the first two throws and so on. These participants expressed that their skills in predicting the next throw correctly were "better than average". This differed from their co-participants who happened to be wrong in the beginning of the study. Thus the participants used past observations to judge their level of perceived uncertainty – despite the fact that they knew better.

Another study was undertaken by Robyn Dawes (1988), who gave his participants the chance to win a lottery. He divided his participants into two groups: one that was handed the lottery ticket and one that was allowed to choose the ticket themselves. The surprising observation in this study was that the people who chose their own lottery ticket stated a higher confidence in having the winning ticket than their co-participants who were simply handed a ticket. It seems that their careful considerations in choosing the ticket influenced their confidence and thus their uncertainty perception. But the extant uncertainty did not change, the probability of winning the lottery and hence having the winning ticket were the same for all participants. Why are these observations so stunning?

The studies give some interesting insights into people's reactions in the face of uncertainty. First, we tend to invent a higher rationale to explain uncertain events. We treat them as if there is a rational reason for the observed outcomes. In the Langer experiment this reason was the "skill" of the participants based on the evidence of true predictions. In the Dawes experiment, the participants had not even had the chance of observing the value of their "skills" and yet they adjusted their perceived uncertainty. The reason these findings are so stunning is that the participants *know* better. They know that their "skills" make no difference to their probability of winning – the probability of predicting the correct throw of the coin or of having the winning lottery ticket experiment stay the same, and yet the participants adjusted their confidence statements.

The reasons for these observations can only be speculative, but researchers believe that this reaction is because we aim to make the outcome of uncertain situations controllable. We hope that we can influence the outcome and thus determine what happens to us. We like to be in control of our own destiny and uncertainty undermines this desire. Thus we often act as if the uncertainty was lower than it actually is or as if it was not there at all. In other words, we often are overconfident.

SURPRISINGLY UNCERTAIN

Because of this overconfidence, we are often surprised when a situation turns out to be more uncertain than we anticipated. This can be captured by the so-called surprise index which is a quantitative measure of the difference between extant and perceived uncertainty when these can be expressed in quantities. Take the example of answering knowledge questions. If you state a confidence level of 80 per cent with your answers but only 7 out of 10 possible answers are correct, your surprise index is 10 per cent (= 80 per cent of the confidence level minus 70 per cent of actually correct answers).

Thus the surprise index gives us a way of measuring how different extant uncertainty is from the perceived uncertainty. It does not only put a number on overconfidence but also predicts if someone is overcautious and thus overestimates the extant uncertainty. Imagine for example you were one of the few people that predicted wrongly every single one of the first few throws in Langer's study. According to the laws of probability, there will be as many people consistently wrong in predicting the first few coin tosses as there will be people being consistently right. However, being one of the few who are wrong often leads us to doubt ourselves and our skills. In this case, you might put a lower confidence value on predicting the next throw, for example 40 per cent. This makes you overcautious, as the surprise index would still be 50 per cent which is lower than the value should be according to your estimate, namely 60 per cent.

The surprise index is thus a good tool to measure overconfidence and over cautiousness. It can measure both sides of deviation from the extant uncertainty. We can even use it when perceived uncertainty and extant uncertainty are the same, that is when a person is neither overconfident nor overcautious. However, the measure has one downside, and that is that it is a measure. We cannot use it in its strict sense when we do not express uncertainty in probabilities but have only words to compare. It is much more difficult to compare a statement of "I am not sure" to what it should be according to the extant uncertainty. The surprise index is very useful but has its limitations when we move towards more real-world situations where uncertainty is expressed in a multitude of ways apart from probabilistic values.

However, it does allow us to evidence some of the phenomena that can be observed when we make decisions under uncertainty. It helped researchers show that we tend to perceive uncertainty differently from what it actually is – even when we know better. This results in many of our decisions being biased either by overconfidence or by over cautiousness.

Attempts at Improving the Situation

Once our reactions to uncertainty have been identified, many researchers asked if it was possible to bring the way we perceive uncertainty closer to the extant uncertainty and thus make it more "correct". The short answer is yes, but not much. The question was again attempted via experiments where participants were asked to give an estimate about an event and attach a confidence level to this estimate. But these experiments have a second round where the participants were informed of their overconfidence before re-entering the game again. The general logic was the following.

Imagine you are a participant in the coin-throwing experiment where you are asked to predict the outcome of the next coin throw and state how confident you are about your prediction being true. If you were one of the lucky participants to have been correct in all of prediction of the first few throws, you may be quite confident in your prediction skills and hence state 70 per cent as your confidence value. So far, so good. Then something new happened. The study leader would let you know that you are overconfident with your estimate and ask you if you wanted to adjust this value. The reaction of most participants was to reduce their statement of confidence to, for example, 65 per cent. Now this is still considerably overconfident, and this despite the fact that the participants knew they were overconfident.

This is quite a stunning finding. In the section above we found that despite knowing better, we tend to attach some form of reasoning or skill to observations that are completely a matter of chance. The result is that we are overconfident or in some cases overcautious. Now we see that even when someone puts the brakes on our decision making and says that we are acting under incorrect assumptions, we do not re-think these assumptions but simply alter them slightly. This is a very interesting observation. We know we are wrong, we are being told that we are wrong, and yet we do not attempt to get it right. We move in the right direction, but essentially we don't change our fundamental behaviour. So what can we do?

Some researchers attempted training their study participants to see if this changed the existence of overconfidence or over cautiousness. We saw that people improve the level of perceived uncertainty when they receive feedback. The researchers argued that if this feedback happens repeatedly, they would eventually come close enough to the expected confidence value. You might by now know what comes next. The participants did adjust their confidence values, but not very much. It took the researchers six rounds of feedback on the confidence values to achieve an improvement of about 50 per cent. In the coin-tossing example, this means after about six rounds of being told that your confidence value is too high, you would adjust your statement to about 60 per cent. This is better than the starting point of 70 per cent but still considerably overconfident.

Reading these papers as an early Ph.D. student, I wondered whether it is possible to "manipulate" the recognition of uncertainty. So I designed what would be the first study of my Ph.D. I assumed that by communicating information visually through for example, graphs or figures, people would be more or less inclined to accept the uncertainty inherent in an estimate. Different graphs accentuate different parts of the available information or the lack of this information. Hence some graphs lead the person who looks at them to recognise the uncertainty it captures while other graphs guide the viewer away from this uncertainty. People who base their decisions on the first set of graphs may have a more realistic perception of the extant uncertainty while those who look at the second set of graphs may be systematically overconfident.

We set out to test this assumption with professionals – with people who did estimations and forecasts in their jobs. We wanted to work with people who knew about the difficulties of predicting events in 5 or 10 years' time and potentially get it wrong. For this we received the support of Arthur Griffiths, then the chairman of SCAF – the Society for Cost Analysis and Forecasting in the UK. SCAF held regular meetings where professional cost estimators and forecasters came together and shared the best practices on the topic. One of these meetings we used for our experiment.

Going about our study design, we faced two challenges. Doing experiments with real-world scenarios has the drawback that the extant uncertainty cannot easily be measured. We said above that in gambling by throwing dice or flipping a coin, the probability of each event can easily be determined. We have a chance of 1 in 6 to throw the number 3 with our dice and a probability of 50 per cent to throw heads with our coin. Thus we can measure the difference between perceived and extant uncertainty via the surprise index, which gives us an accurate measure of by how much someone is overconfident or overcautious. In the real world, this is often not the case. Thus, in real-world decision scenarios there is no obvious "right" or "wrong" in our expressed confidence values. The only thing we can judge is how realistic the confidence value seems in light of the available information.

Another challenge with real-world scenarios is the time difference between when we make a decision and when we can observe the outcome of this decision. This is important as we can only judge the difference between extant and perceived uncertainty when we receive feedback of what actually happened. In the experiments described above, the outcome could be observed immediately. Rolling the dice, we can see whether we threw the number 3 or not. Flipping a coin, we can see whether we have heads or tails. In real-world scenarios, these observations are often not immediately available. Sometimes we may be able to make observations after a few months, sometimes only after decades, but almost always the resolution does not come immediately.

Hence real-world decisions are a bit trickier to investigate in experimental studies. In my study, we decided to test three graphical displays of cost forecasts typically used in practice. These three displays were a three-point trend forecast, a bar chart with maximum and minimum values around the mean value, and a fan diagram with confidence values for intervals around the mean value. You can see the figures in Figure 2.2. The figures were all based on the same data and showed the same information but differed in the way this information was displayed.

At one of SCAF's meetings, Arthur allowed us to do our study with the costing experts. We divided them into three groups, each of which received one of the displays shown above. In this way, we could compare the experts' responses to the three displays. What we found was quite remarkable.

The approach to displaying the uncertainty around the available information impacted the confidence levels and the line of reasoning the experts gave for their estimates. Specifically, the fan diagram made them attach lower confidence levels to their estimates than the other two graphs. The fan diagram made the experts more aware of the uncertainty and they gave this more frequently as a reason for their decision making. In addition, we observed these reactions without making them aware that it was the perceived uncertainty we were interested in. This means we can be relatively confident that they did not simply pay us lip service by showing these reactions.

The limitations to experimenting with real-world scenarios instead of games meant that we could not compare our findings to extant uncertainty.

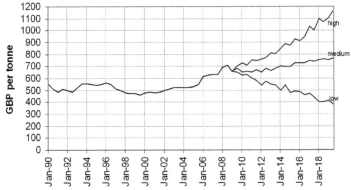
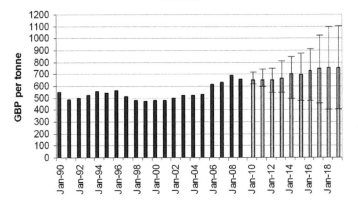

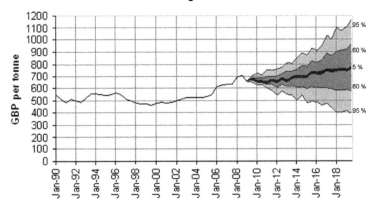

FIGURE 2.2 THREE APPROACHES TO DISPLAYING UNCERTAINTY: (A) THREE-POINT TREND FORECAST; (B) A BAR CHART; (C) A FAN DIAGRAM

This means that we could not judge whether the different figures impacted the level of overconfidence or over cautiousness. However, the findings do give an interesting and important indication that we can in fact impact the perception of uncertainty and that graphical information is one approach to doing exactly that.

Why are these observations so special? They suggest that we can be manipulated in recognising and accepting uncertainty. In combination with the studies shown above, our study suggests that we need to be manipulated to accept uncertainty because we tend to underestimate it and be overconfident. We do not change significantly if someone tells us we are overconfident, but we do change significantly if someone re-directs us into acknowledging uncertainty without our explicit knowledge of it.

The answers to the questions posed at the beginning of this chapter are the British and jaundice.

CHAPTER 3

Expressing Uncertainty

What is the name of the comic strip character that eats spinach to increase his strength?

What is the name of the submarine in Jules Verne's *20,000 Leagues Beneath the Sea*?

What is the name of the brightest star in the sky excluding the sun?

If you are like me, you do not know the answer to at least one of these questions. You may formulate your answer differently to the questions that you are not so sure of such as "could this be ... ?" or "maybe this was ... ?" You may also hesitate and think before you give your answer. There are many ways you can show and express that you are uncertain about your answers, and this expression varies depending on our level of uncertainty. The response may also differ depending how much we want to appear as knowledgeable and thus certain (i.e. not uncertain).

Text, Noise and Show

When we make a statement that we are uncertain about, we tend to indicate this in various ways. When I am asked by a friend for example whether they should be taking an umbrella with them the next day, my response can include multiple facets that indicate how uncertain I am about my answer. As I typically do not watch the weather forecast, my first reaction could be to shrug my shoulders because I don't know the best answer. And then I might start explaining what I would do if I was in my friend's position. "Maybe stay close to shelter if you prefer to not take an umbrella. If that is possible? Just in case it does rain ... " Saying something like this, my voice would also indicate the uncertainty, sounding quite vague in making any suggestion.

We express uncertainty in various ways – through what we say, how we say it and what gestures or movements we make to accompany our statement. In other words, we have textual, audio and visual cues for indicating that we are uncertain. When we interpret what another person means, we usually take all of these factors into account. Sometimes what is being said is most important, at other times the subtle differences come from *how* it is said. Thus we express our perceived uncertainty about something in what we say, how we sound and how we look when we say it.

What I Say and What I Mean

Most research has focused on analysing the content of what it is we say in certain situations. The reason for this is clear; it is the most accessible part of our language. We can write down exactly what is being said so we can later analyse it. Many analysis methods have been developed to understand when certain terms are used, what they indicate and what they mean. One of these methods is content analysis where researchers look at the frequency of certain words in a written text to discern the meaning of the conveyed message. With content analysis, we can investigate underlying meanings and themes in books, published articles, announcements, transcripts of speeches, political talks and interviews, even of songs and other cultural media. We can also let multiple analysts use the methods to see how much they agree on their findings. Using the content of what is being said offers a lot of basis for researchers for their analyses.

NUMBERS VS DESCRIPTIONS

We can articulate uncertainty in two fundamentally different ways: quantitatively through numbers and qualitatively through words. Quantitative uncertainty expresses the uncertainty we can measure, for example as spreads or in probabilities. This gives the advantage that we can model the information including the related uncertainty. I used the output of such a model in my experimental study with the professional cost estimators of SCAF presented in Chapter 2. Another advantage of quantitative uncertainty is that we can easily judge its meaning. A probability of 50 per cent is smaller than a probability of 60 per cent. This made it an easy approach for the research establishing the link between extant and perceived uncertainty described in Chapter 2, because we can easily see if someone is overconfident. Quantitative uncertainty expression offers a lot of advantages and has thus received most attention by researchers.

The problem is that in most of our statements we do not use quantitative expressions. We usually express our uncertainty in qualitative statements.

How often do I say that I am "30 per cent certain" that something will happen or that I am "70 per cent sure" to do something next week? Almost never. Usually, I would describe these confidence values with somewhat fuzzier but more natural words. I would say that something is "unlikely" or "likely", that something is "not quite clear" or that I have "not decided yet". So we use specific expressions to indicate our uncertainty about a situation.

In some situations we need a quantitative value but only have qualitative assessments available. This happens in a lot of real-world situations, for example when we only have some experts available to judge a situation. This has been captured in the preference paradox which states that people like to give qualitative uncertainty statements such as "probable" but like to receive numerical probability statements such as "70 per cent". This means that we need to convert expert assessments of a situation – which are often given in qualitative uncertainty statements – into numbers so that decision makers and managers can use them in their assessment.

One example is when medical doctors assess the likelihood that a certain symptom is the sign of a specific illness. For these situations, researchers have tried to link different qualitative uncertainty expressions to their quantitative equivalent. For example, the research team around Silja Renooij and Cilia Witteman (1999) developed and tested a scale for transferring qualitative statements into probability values. Their field of application was medicine where doctors were presented with different symptoms which by themselves or in combination with each other could be linked to a certain illness. Using various tests with different people, the research team refined and validated their scale. I have used such a scale in my research to elicit expert opinion on different cost factors, a fundamentally different area to that of Renooij and Witteman. And I found the approach very useful indeed.

The underlying logic of linking qualitative statements to probabilistic values is that a term such as "probable" indicates a different confidence level than the term "unexpected". They started by finding some suitable terms that could be represented in such a conversion chart. The difficulty was the large amount of available terms that can indicate uncertainty, as an event can range from "remote" or "highly improbable" to "reasonably possible", "expected" or even "virtually certain". Thus various terms are useful in different contexts. For example, the Financial Accounting Standard SFAS 5 – a standard approach used for reporting companies' financial performance and forecasts – defined three terms that are to be used to assess the uncertainty in auditing: "probable", "reasonably possible" and "remote". Researchers around the world have tested these three terms with varying numbers and characteristics of participants using both practitioners as students. The results of these studies are very interesting.

The first finding that is shown time and time again in the different studies is that the interpretation of qualitative uncertainty statements into numbers is problematic and differs highly between individuals. The second is that qualitative uncertainty statements are less precise than numerical statements. That means that a qualitative term such as "probable" can be related to an interval of quantitative values. Ning Du and Kevin Stevens (2011) did exactly this – linking the three terms "probable", "reasonably possible" and "remote" to quantitative probability values. Their results are shown in Figure 3.1. In comparison, the SFAS 5 official definitions of the terms are:

- Probable: the future event is likely to happen.
- Reasonably possible: the chance of the future event happening is somewhere between remote and probable.
- Remote: the chance of the future event happening is slight.

The figure shows not only that the numerical translations of the three qualitative statements are fuzzy and ambiguous, but also that they partly

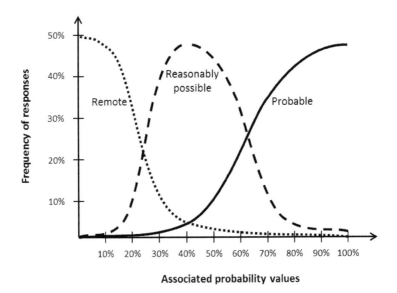

Associated probability values

FIGURE 3.1 ASSOCIATION OF SPECIFIC QUALITATIVE UNCERTAINTY TERMS WITH NUMERICAL PROBABILITY VALUES

overlap. This means their numerical interpretation is not as clear-cut as the definitions provided by SFAS 5 suggest. And the larger the number of qualitative uncertainty terms, the more difficult their interpretation because the numerical associations will overlap substantially. Yet some form of conversion is needed in order to translate qualitative into quantitative assessments (and vice versa).

Renooij and Witteman developed these insights further. They created a transformation scale that they could use when they talked to their experts and asked them about their assessments of future uncertain events. Once they found some terms that were useful in their context, they had to link them to appropriate probabilistic values. The meaning of words is somewhat fuzzier than the meaning of a number. For example, a qualitative term such as "probable" cannot simply be linked to a probabilistic number such as 80 per cent. Rather, we link it to an interval of probabilistic values. After various studies, their conversion chart was presentable. Figure 3.2 shows such a conversion chart, and this is the one I used in my research.

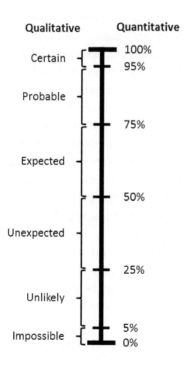

FIGURE 3.2 TRANSFORMATION BETWEEN QUALITATIVE AND QUANTITATIVE UNCERTAINTY EXPRESSIONS

The conversion chart can be used when asking experts about their assessment of uncertain links – or eliciting subjective probabilities. Imagine that a researcher like me asked you about tomorrow's weather in your town. Neither of us has access to a professional weather forecast but I ask you because I am new in town and you have lived there for some time. So you know what the conditions are, how the weather has been over recent weeks and if it switches quickly. You are the expert and I am interested in your (uncertain) opinion. I present you with a conversion chart as shown above – which you can use or choose to ignore. If you use it, I will translate the statements into quantitative values as presented in the chart. If you say that it is probably going to rain in the morning, I will give this statement a probabilistic value of 75–95 per cent. Thus the chart gives me a way to transfer your descriptions into numbers which I could use for further modelling and simulations.

WORDS AND PHRASES

We can also assess the use of language in more detail to understand the uncertainty it expresses. In our language, we use different words and phrases that indicate when we are uncertain about the content of what we are saying. This linguistic phenomenon has been called hedges. We use hedges to make our statements fuzzier or blur the exact meaning of a word or a phrase. Compare the statements given in Figure 3.3. Their content is (more or less) the same between the left- and right-hand sides. The first line statements all communicate the weather situation in Copenhagen – this is the core message. But the level of uncertainty connected with the statements is different. The sentences on the right include a degree of uncertainty which we can detect by the words that are added around the core message. These words are hedges. Their task is to blur the core message and they are used by someone who is uncertain about the core message.[1]

With hedges, the truth value of our statement cannot be ascertained. It is relatively easy to say whether the statement "it rains in Copenhagen" is right or wrong. But when I say "I think it may rain in Copenhagen", I cannot be proved wrong (or right). What I think is in my head and the existence of my thoughts

---

1   The use of hedges is not limited to indicating a person's uncertainty about a core message. In Great Britain for example, hedges are used for more or less every statement, from social situations of having a coffee with friends to work situations of discussing an idea or a plan. This has led to various jokes about what a British person says in contrast to what a non-British person understands they mean.

Without hedges	With hedges
It rains in Copenhagen.	<u>I think</u> it <u>may</u> rain in Copenhagen.
Paul likes to eat berries.	<u>According to</u> his mother, Paul likes to eat berries.
A cup of coffee costs 2.65 €.	A cup of coffee costs <u>about</u> 3 €.
The girl's dress is yellow.	The girl's dress is <u>somewhat</u> yellow.

FIGURE 3.3 EXEMPLARY USES OF HEDGES

cannot be easily judged to be correct. The truth value of this statement cannot be ascertained – at least not that easily.

Different terms indicate different linguistic phenomena. The underlined terms in Figure 3.3 fulfil different purposes when blurring the core message. We have words that *shield* the message. Shields are terms that blur the plausibility or attribution of the core message. The phrases "I think" or "I believe" are shields. So are phrases that attribute the source of the core message to someone or something else. For example, when we use "according to … " we basically say that what follows is something that we heard or read somewhere and thus cannot be attributed to us. These words shield the core message by blurring its meaning.

Another way of hedging is to use approximators. Approximators give a ballpark rather than an exact statement. For example, I may be uncertain of the exact cost of a cup of coffee, but I may know that it is "around" a certain price. Similar terms can adapt the meaning of a sentence, such as "a little bit" or "somewhat". These words approximate the truth value of our core message by blurring its meaning.

We use hedges regularly in our conversations. Comparing different means of communicating, researchers have tried to find out what other purposes the use of hedges can have. They found that we are most likely to use them in personal, face-to-face conversations. We use them much less often in indirect conversations via the Internet, emails or letters, for example. This means that hedges do not just indicate uncertainty, they are also used for the purpose of conversational flow or being polite. One typical example is that a lot of my British friends would not simply say "No" when they disagree with a statement I make, but would rather say that "this *could* be the case". They would use a hedge out of politeness, not because they are uncertain. Thus, hedges are one indicator of uncertainty but not a clear indicator because they can also be attributed to other functions in our language.

Another phenomenon is the weasel. Weasels are animals that are believed to take their nutrition from other animals' eggs,[2] and they do this quite impressively by sucking the content out of the egg and leaving the shell intact. So they leave an egg that at first sight appears normal but is completely hollow inside. In a linguistic sense, weasels are sentence constructions that can be used when there is uncertainty around a fact. We use them for example when the source of the information is not known or uncertain. Weasel words are intended to make a statement sound more legitimate and impressive. An example is a sentence in the passive: The chocolate was eaten. The fact is there, but the core of the message is missing. We still do not know who did it. Another example is "people say that ... ". No one knows exactly who and it cannot be proven wrong or right – you simply may not have asked the right kind of people when checking the statement. We leave things out of the sentence, thus we commit a weasel.

HOW MUCH I KNOW

What we say and the terms we use to say it indicates the degree to which we are uncertain about our statement. One way to judge the degree of uncertainty is the inherent meaning of words. For example, when we state a possible event in the future, we can use the phrases "going to" and "will". By definition, the phrase "I am going to do something" describes a plan and thus indicates a lower degree of uncertainty than the phrase "I will do something". Similarly, the words "might" and "may" indicate different levels of uncertainty by their inherent meanings.

Another way to assess the degree of uncertainty is the clustering of words and phrases that indicate uncertainty. I can use one or multiple hedges in one sentence and the more terms or phrases I use, the higher the degree of uncertainty. Some of the phrases in the Figure 3.3 use multiple hedges and each of these terms indicates some uncertainty. The multiplicity of terms indicates a higher degree of uncertainty. We can thus use the content of what we say as an indication of the degree of uncertainty of the speaker.

---

2   This is actually not proven but was a widespread belief for centuries. This is where the meaning of weasel words comes from and I suppose it includes the insult of being a weasel.

How I Sound

Similar to the content of our statement, the tone of it can indicate our uncertainty. The amount of insights that research offers in this field is much thinner than suggestions on the content of our messages. One reason for this may be that it is much harder to judge this link for audio cues. We need audio recordings of the statements, and tools for methodically analysing audio recordings are not as easily available. This is a problem for researchers because the findings can potentially be biased and not reproducible. Thus there are few conclusive findings in this area.

Audio cues of uncertainty can be various. For example, the intonation of a sentence may be different when we feel uncertain. The pitch at the end of the sentence may increase in a similar way to when we ask a question. This intonation typically asks for some reaction in our conversation partner regarding the correctness of our statement. Increasing the pitch at the end of a sentence indicates that this is not a final thought, and thus there is some uncertainty in our statement.

Similarly, when a person is uncertain about what they say, they are more likely to produce pauses and have delays in responding to a question or a comment of their conversation partner. We are hesitant about our statement because we are uncertain about it and its level of correctness. Have you ever been asked a question where you were not sure about the correct answer? When this happens to me, I tend to pause for a bit – usually because I desperately try to think what the correct answer could be – and then I answer. And when I answer, my voice tends to be less intense – I speak more softly and with less conviction. These phenomena can indicate uncertainty.

How I Look

Our mimic and gestures can also express if we are uncertain about what we say. We give visual cues that complement what we say and how we say it. For example, people who are uncertain about their statement were found to be more likely to raise their eyebrows when they say something. They may also be giving an embarrassed or excusing smile and are more likely to make specific head movements. These may be expressions of uncertainty when we say something, but are they exclusive signs of uncertainty?

As I stated before, research in the areas of audio and visual cues for uncertainty is in its infancy compared to how the content of our statements indicate uncertainty. Thus these observations have been made in very specific circumstances. The studies are based on tested people's factual knowledge – similar to the questions at the beginning of this chapter. The situations were thus that the experiment facilitator would ask them a factual question to which the respondent did or did not know the answer. The respondent thus had a degree of (un)certainty in their statement. The situation is such that the respondent may be exposed as to their ignorance, which puts some pressure on them. Most of us care about our self-presentation and do not want to be exposed as ignorant. We may thus feel pressure and be nervous when we are put in such a situation and our reactions express this accordingly.

Reactions to factual questions are relatively rare in the real world in comparison to natural dialogues or discussions. In reality, we may show some of the described behaviours even when we are not uncertain. We may raise our intonation at the end of the sentence to signal that we intend to follow up on this statement or we may raise our eyebrows to emphasis the point we are trying to make. Next time someone gives an answer you expect them to be uncertain about, have a look at their expressions and see what they tell you.

Popeye, Nautilus and Sirius. These are the answers to the questions from the beginning of this chapter.

CHAPTER 4

Accepting Uncertainty

Few of us would give up a stable and safe career for anything. Once we have done the training, we know what we are doing, we have sufficient experience to deal with unexpected events and feedback and most importantly, we know (roughly) what is lying ahead. Once we have created this silo of certainty around us, it is difficult to let go of it. Few of us throw our career achievements away to start over again in a different field, or even worse, to create a career path that has not existed before. Just the thought of uncertainty can make us tremble with fear and insecurity.

Some people, however, welcome uncertainty in their lives and challenge themselves to embrace uncertainty and conquer new career paths. One such person is Randy Komisar. Having taken a more than impressive career path from being a lawyer to running LucasArts Entertainment to becoming the CEO of Crystal Dynamics, he was bound to bigger challenges in his future. He could have directed his career towards becoming a CEO of a bigger company, gaining more prestige and reputation. But he noticed that he did not like this path and he decided to do something different.

He decided to leave Crystal Dynamics. "I bailed out of an airplane that was still in midair" as he recalls this experience himself. He decided to welcome uncertainty into his life – to embrace the unknown future. He left the "safe path" of his career to do something different. He freed himself from the constraints of expectations of success and he saw opportunities where before was safety.

He created a new career path – the Virtual CEO – a set of personal qualities and experience that he had and that was needed in Silicon Valley during the 1990s start-up boom. The entrepreneurs at this time were not experienced enough to build businesses. Komisar partnered with entrepreneurs to lead their newly established organisations and help them grow their businesses with everything this entails: strategy, recruiting, partnering with suppliers and other organisations, financing and leadership. "I served as consigliere without displacing them" is how he describes it.

For most of us, the situation Randy Komisar placed himself in would be frightening, inducing anxiety about our very existence. For him, it was exhilarating, energising. However, most of us accept some levels of uncertainty in our everyday lives. For example, crossing that main street on the way to work is affiliated with some level of uncertainty. So are activities such as driving a car, meeting new people and answering general knowledge questions. These are instances where we regularly accept uncertainty and deal with it. In other situations, we may not be so tolerant of the existence of uncertainty. This is what we will look at in this chapter: when do we accept uncertainty and how do we experience its existence?

The Two Faces of Uncertainty

In general, we can have two fundamentally different attitudes towards accepting uncertainty: we may embrace it, or we may want to avoid it as much as possible. Researchers have also highlighted these two different ways of experiencing uncertainty. On the one hand, we find papers using positive metaphors such as

- Uncertainty as growth and the certainty being affiliated with a lack of growth
- Uncertainty is the "bread and butter" of certain professions such as statistics
- Uncertainty as a source for inspiration, artistic freedom and creativity.

On the other hand, negative metaphors have been used in connection to uncertainty, such as;

- blurring the truth
- crippling decision making and taking actions
- highlighting certainty as the Holy Grail.

Researchers in psychology have looked at how people experience the existence of uncertainty. They found that the willingness to accept uncertainty is an individual trait: some people are willing and able to accept higher levels of uncertainty than others. And some people experience uncertainty more pleasantly than others. The researchers differentiated two fundamentally different reactions. Some people feel overwhelmed in situations of high uncertainty, even paralysed. They may not be able to make a decision or act. Others found the situation encouraging and were able to find new solutions and answers to situations they had not experienced before. Why do we react so differently to uncertainty?

CONTROL

One factor causing this difference of accepting uncertainty was the perception of controlling the situation and the uncertainty inherent to it. Control is the ability to cope with a situation. If I have a high level of control, I can impact everything that is happening around me. If I have low levels of control, things simply happen to me without my active influence. Thus control describes if I can attribute the outcome of an event to myself and my abilities and skills or if it is completely down to luck.

When a situation offers a high level of control, individuals can feel more intrinsic motivation and show more initiative. This is caused by factors such as greater interest, less pressure, more creativity and a higher self-esteem. For example, if you are given a task you had not done before but you know you have the skills to complete it, you may be very motivated in achieving your goal. You may even be so motivated that you work an extensive period of time and do not rest until you find a viable solution. In contrast, when a situation offers a low level of control we are less likely to experience this motivation, creativity and self-esteem. We may be more inclined to feel dread and describe the situation in its catastrophic potential.

In a study aimed at participants of different cultural background, Li-Jun Ji, Kaiping Peng and Richard Nisbett introduced the possibility of control into an experimental study. The study participants were asked to make choices based on uncertain scenarios. In this experiment, the researchers allowed the participants to control the progress of the study scenario by clicking a key on the keyboard. This had a very interesting effect on the uncertainty perception of these participants. Their expressed confidence levels for their decisions increased. In other words, the more control the participants perceived they had of a situation, the less uncertainty they associated with it. This highlights an interesting link between the two concepts.

This is a relatively intuitive finding. The more I feel I can influence the outcome of a situation, the less uncertain I feel about it. When my boss gives me a deadline for next week and I feel it is completely up to me to finish the necessary work by then, this deadline has me less worried. If, on the other hand, I am dependent on many other people to achieve the necessary work– I may need signatures, information from previous projects and so on – I may be more worried about the deadline and feel much more uncertain about reaching my goals in the given time. This link between emotions and uncertainty is another interesting area of study.

EMOTIONS AND UNCERTAINTY

"Fear, hope and surprise are distinguished from the other emotions by uncertainty." This statement was made by Craig Smith and Phoebe Ellsworth based on a study of how people experience different emotions in their lives. Situations that contain uncertainty cause different emotional responses in us. We may feel fear, hope, or surprise; we may also feel anxiety or frustration. These anticipatory emotions can be the immediate responses to the existence of uncertainty. In contrast, we may also feel anticipated emotions which we may expect to experience in the future and are thus not immediate. We may feel regret about a missed opportunity, rejoicing about a gain or disappointment about some financial loss. We are particularly interested in anticipatory emotions here as the immediate responses in situations of uncertainty.

Anticipatory emotions encode a summary of what we see as the possible consequences of an action or inaction. It is what we often describe as our gut feeling. We are confident about crossing that main road on the way to work every day because our anticipatory emotions tell us that there is no or low levels of danger there. In contrast, we do not want to make a certain investment because we fear the possibility of losing a large amount of money. In reality, many of our decisions are a trade-offs between different considerations. In terms of emotions, this may embark on a trade-off between greed and fear. Anticipatory emotions play a central role in our decision making and we will get back to the nature of this role in Chapter 5, Deciding under uncertainty.

In their work on emotions, Smith and Ellsworth surveyed different people on situations in which they have felt these emotions and asked them to describe these situations regarding various factors, one of which was the perception of uncertainty. They subsequently ranked the emotions on a scale between certain and uncertain which is shown in Figure 4.1. They found that emotions differ with regard to the level of uncertainty we perceive in the situation.

Surprise and fear are two of the most uncertain emotions we feel. In surprising situations, the study participants described that they felt more uncertain than in any other situation and that they experienced a strong desire to attend to the situation and do something about it. Surprises are usually caused by others – we rarely surprise ourselves. Imagine for example that you receive an unexpected present for your birthday – say a voucher for a spa holiday – you get flowers from your boyfriend or you receive an A for a test you

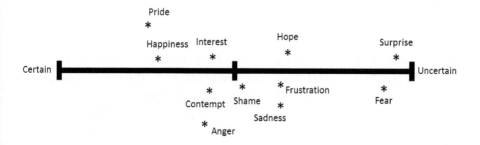

FIGURE 4.1 EMOTIONS BETWEEN CERTAINTY AND UNCERTAINTY

expected a C for. These are all situations of surprise and we usually want to do something about it – tell our friends and family, book that holiday into our calendars or make sure the flowers are attended to.

Fear on the other hand is usually not accompanied by a strong desire to do something. It is thus in some regards the other side of the coin of surprise as it is also typically experienced in very uncertain situations. The uncertainty is typically associated with a lack of knowing whether we will be able to escape the situation or avoid an unpleasant outcome. We can have a fear of public speaking, for example, or of flying.

Smith and Ellsworth characterise the other emotions shown in Figure 4.1. The point I would like to make here is that uncertainty can be associated with both pleasant and unpleasant emotions. We can be surprised or experience fear in uncertain situations. Thus our emotional reaction may be both positive and negative. However, negative feelings tend to dominate the positive ones. That is to say, avoiding the possibility of negative feelings typically motivates us more than the possibility of positive feelings does. We are more inclined to act for avoiding negative outcomes than we are for achieving positive ones.

Daniel Kahneman and Amos Tversky described this observation in Prospect Theory. The theory says this: we experience losses more severely than we experience the same gain. Their theory measures these losses and gain in monetary terms. The translation of these predictions in terms of emotions is only possible to a limited degree; however, the overall logic stands. This is probably why the experience of uncertainty as a threat and its association with emotions such as fear or anxiety has received much higher attention in the literature than the experience of uncertainty as an opportunity that is associated with positive emotions.

Experiencing Uncertainty as a Threat

Most academic theories classify uncertainty as a threat that needs to be reduced, resolved or overturned. The less uncertainty, the better. The typical assumption is that uncertainty has a negative impact on people – they experience fear, anxiety or insecurity under uncertainty – and thus invariably try to avoid it. One explanation for this is given by Prospect Theory, already mentioned above. Prospect Theory explains how we experience the prospect of an uncertain loss or gain. It places the starting point of our evaluations at the current situation – meaning that we compare any uncertain outcome against the status quo, the situation as it is before the decision. We then evaluate the possibility of a monetary gain in comparison to a monetary loss.

The core part of the theory is that we experience the prospect of a loss more severely than we experience the prospect of a gain. If you had the option of participating in a game with two distinct outcomes: if you win, you will receive €100, if you lose you will have to pay €100. Prospect Theory states that you will experience the fear of losing €100 more severely than you will experience the joy of receiving €100. Figure 4.2 presents this core message in a graphic form.

This graph is an approximation over various people. You can imagine each individual forming a specific line within the graph. Some people might even value gains more severely than losses, but overall – that is to say over a large amount of people Kahneman and Tversky studied when formulating this theory – we tend to be more afraid of losses than we anticipate gains. We can see this is as one possible explanation for the vast majority of research highlighting the negative experience of uncertainty.

REDUCING AND AVOIDING UNCERTAINTY

Uncertain situations may evoke the feeling of a lack of control and cause us to delay or avoid making a decision when we do not have enough information. We may experience immediacies as certainties and delays as uncertainties that can be avoided. One example for this phenomenon comes again from psychology research. In experimental studies, participants were threatened with the possibility of an electrical shock as a punishment. The further this possible electrical shock was predicted to be into the future, the less strong the emotional response of the participant. This shows that we experience more immediate uncertain outcomes more severely than if they are further in the future.

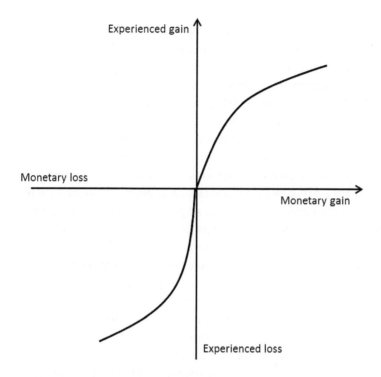

FIGURE 4.2 PROSPECT OF GAINS AND LOSSES

Much research highlights that we are willing and motivated to reduce uncertainty. This motivation arises from the felt need to defend again threatening aspects of reality. If you did not know the answer to some of the knowledge questions mentioned in Chapters 2 and 3, you may have looked the answer up by now. You were made aware of your uncertainty and used this as a motivation to reduce the uncertainty.

UNCERTAINTY AS INSECURITY

Uncertainty may be experienced as insecurity. The immediate psychological result of being in a new situation is a lack of security. This insecurity is thus a negative association with an uncertain situation. Imaging, for example, that you are meeting with a person you have never met before – a business meeting or a job interview. You are uncertain about this person as you have no knowledge about them – their sense of humour, level of experience, focus of expertise, their attitude towards you or their interests. If this person also has a background in a different culture, you may further be uncertain as to the customs of greeting them, raising points or explaining your opinion. You are uncertain with regard to the best action in this situation.

This situation has been captured in the so-called uncertainty reduction theory. As its name suggests, we are motivated to reducing our uncertainty within initial social interactions in order to increase our comfort level in dealing with other people. We may start reducing our uncertainty by inquiring about the other person's interests to find some similarities with ourselves. Or we may want to stir the dialogue into an area we are more comfortable with because we know something about it. These are all possibilities that reduce our perceived uncertainty and aim at making us feel more secure in such situations.

This is not always the case – we do not get to know everyone we meet better so that we can reduce our perceived uncertainty and insecurity. There are specific conditions under which we engage in such behaviour. One such condition is whether we expect to see that person again in the future. We are more inclined to become less uncertain about someone we anticipate meeting again – a friend of a new boy or girlfriend, for example, or a new colleague in a firm we have just joined. Another condition is whether the other person has control over us or over something we want. That is to say we are more inclined to reduce our uncertainty regarding someone who interviews us for a new job than we are regarding a stranger who asks us about the time on the street.

This suggests that the predictions of uncertainty reduction theory do not always hold true. We are not always inclined to get to know someone better and reduce our perceived uncertainty and experienced insecurity. There are situations when we accept uncertainty as a given part of our daily lives and we will investigate this side of uncertainty later on in this chapter. But first, let us turn to an even more radical negative experience of uncertainty.

FEAR AND ANXIETY

Uncertainty can make us feel fear and even anxiety. Some authors have highlighted that anxiety is the emotional consequence of uncertainty or even the emotional equivalence of uncertainty. They found that the existence of uncertainty can cause the same physiological signs as anxiety. We experience fear or anxiety in many situations – sometimes to a lower degree than at other times. Sometimes we experience it as feeling uneasy, tense, worried or apprehensive about what might happen. When we feel fear, we tend to take rather extreme actions. As George Loewenstein put it "fear causes us to slam the brakes, it immobilises us when we have the greatest need for strength" (2001, p. 271). Thus fear and anxiety are very powerful anticipatory emotional responses to the existence of uncertainty.

People often feel powerful fears of outcomes that they recognise to be highly unlikely – such as an airplane crash or a terrorist attack – or not objectively terrible, for example public speaking. The focus in these situations is often on the debilitating consequences of uncertainty. We highlight the unpredictability and uncontrollability of these events in our minds. Again, time plays an important role. The closer this aversive uncertain situation, the larger our fear of it.

Fear is one of the emotions that Smith and Ellsworth identified as arising in highly uncertain situations. It has a strong link to the level of control we hold in this situation: we tend to experience fear in situations where we lack control. Thus, we feel fear when we are unsure if we can escape or avoid an unpleasant outcome. One example is the fear of terrorism and the future plans involving terrorist activities. Being the target of a terrorist acts is highly unlikely for you and me, in fact, much less likely than dying in a car accident, for example. And yet many of us are terrified of terrorist activities. This fear in us is one of the goals of terrorist activities and the perpetrators specifically speculate on its powerful influence on our decision and actions.

Despite the hypothesis that anxiety and uncertainty may be two sides of the same coin, other researchers have only found a moderate link between the two concepts. From their findings, anxiety arises particularly from a lack of predictability and a lack of trust in other people. For example, imagine you meet someone for the first time and you thus do not know their personality, interests, likely actions and whether they like you or not. This someone could be the person interviewing you for the job you would really like or the parents of your new boy or girlfriend. Research says we tend to feel some degree of anxiety because we are not able to predict how this person may act or react to us.

Experiencing it as an Opportunity

In some circumstances, uncertainty gives rise to a lot of opportunities and thus positive emotions. As stated above, this side of uncertainty has been largely ignored by researchers yet it is so important in our daily lives and how we experience different situations. Emotional responses to uncertainty can also include positive feelings such as hope, thrill or exhilaration. Thus uncertainty gives rise to a lot of possibilities and we may experience the existence of these possibilities in various different emotional responses. I would like to explore a few points in this section to highlight the second side of accepting uncertainty in our lives.

EMBRACING THE EXPERIENCE

Some individuals may purposefully seek uncertainty or accept chronically elevated uncertainty. These are people who purposefully seek novel information and novel experiences and are open to full and honest communication. They tolerate uncertainty well because they see it as an opportunity to gain new knowledge and are not defensive about prior beliefs. These people tend to be more oriented towards uncertainty in their lives.

Milton Rokeach (1960) described people that fit this description as "gestalt types". Rokeach's research focused on social psychology. He defined the existence of different personalities on a continuum like the one shown in Figure 4.3. On the one extreme are what he called gestalt types: people who Rokeach describes as being open minded because they possess a cognitive belief system that is oriented towards new beliefs and new information. On the other extreme are psychoanalytic types of people who are more closed minded because they possess cognitive belief systems that are oriented towards familiar and predictable events. In impressive amounts of studies, he links these personality types to differences in prejudice, cognitive problem solving, music appreciation and political and religious opinion. Thus gestalt types are less prejudiced, less authoritarian, less religiously dogmatic, more politically

Gestalt type	Psychoanalytic type
• Need for a cognitive framework to know and understand; • Open minded • Possesses cognitive belief system oriented toward new beliefs and/or information	• Need to ward off threatening aspects of reality; • Close minded • Possesses cognitive belief system oriented toward familiar and/or predictable events

FIGURE 4.3 GESTALT AND PSYCHOANALYTIC TYPES OF PERSONS

progressive, better at problem solving and more artistically appreciative. And subsequently – and most importantly for the focus of this book – gestalt types tend to be more accepting and even seeking of uncertainty.

In these circumstances, uncertainty may also give rise to creativity. Take for example the performing arts. The uncertainty in interpreting musical compositions gives the musician the freedom to use their creativity. One extreme of this creativity can be seen in the improvisations of jazz musicians who play without any precomposed musical guide. But creativity also has a place in many other parts of our lives, and the existence of uncertainty is a crucial enabler of this creativity.

HOPE AND SURPRISE

Uncertainty can also give rise to positive anticipatory emotions such as hope and surprise. In Smith and Ellsworth's research, these two emotions were highly correlated with experienced uncertainty. Simply speaking, surprise arises from uncertainty about what is happening and hope is uncertainty about what may happen in the future.

When we are surprised we usually have no control over the situation. In Smith and Ellsworth's studies, the participants reported that surprises were always caused by other people. Someone does something we did not expect them to do. A grumpy boss suddenly thanks you for work well done, your spouse surprises you with a breakfast in bed or your children bring home an A in a subject they usually struggle with. Feeling surprised tends to also come along with a strong desire to attend to the situation. We tell our colleagues about our boss's reaction, we may offer to cook dinner in return for our spouse or we hang the test results up on the fridge.

When we are hopeful, we build on the knowledge that it is possible but not certain that we get what we want. As a child, we may have been hoping for that special present for Christmas. Later we may have been hoping for a place in the university we really wanted to go to. These anticipatory emotions are only possible in situations where uncertainty is present.

TRUST

Another positive feeling that is connected to uncertainty is trust. We can only trust someone if we have some level of uncertainty about their possible actions.

Only the possibility of opportunistic behaviour gives value to trusting another person not to engage in this behaviour. Thus trust is an expectation of another person that alleviates the fear that a partner – a romantic partner, a friend, a child, a family member – will act opportunistically. Trust is a particular level of subjective probability. It defines our personal assessment of someone else's likely behaviour.

We often base our trust on the knowledge we have about another person, but trust also needs a remaining level of uncertainty. This uncertainty arises from the fundamental inability to completely and perfectly predict other people's behaviour. I cannot even completely predict my own behaviour. Sometimes, when I am asked to explain how I would react in a certain situation, I find it difficult to respond because unless I am in this situation, the discussion remains on a hypothetical level. Unless a situation becomes real, it is difficult to say how I would react. Similarly, I cannot predict how other people will react. This uncertainty about other's behaviour is where trust plays an important role in enabling and enforcing personal social relationships.

CHAPTER 5
Deciding under Uncertainty

On 22 October 2012, the court in the Italian city of L'Aquila came to a decision that would shake the scientific community around the world. This decision convicted seven members of the National Commission for the Forecast and Prevention of Major Risks of manslaughter after 309 people were killed by an earthquake on 6 April 2009. The charges were that the experts failed to properly assess and communicate the risk of an earthquake in the area as they provided "inaccurate, incomplete and contradictory" information. The experts gave falsely reassuring statements prior to the quake; one committee member was reported to have stated that there was no danger from the tremors at all. This led the residents of L'Aquila to stay and fail to prepare.

Scientifically, none of the signs would have led scientists to predict a major earthquake for the area. Only 2 per cent of small tremors lead to a major quake, yet with a measurement of 5.8 to 5.9 on the Richter scale, the L'Aquila earthquake was exactly such a major event. The experts simply focused on the most likely outcome (no major earthquake) rather than including the uncertainty. The uncertainty around predicting earthquakes is large and a major quake was always a possibility. Ignoring this uncertainty proved fatal for many residents of L'Aquila, yet the seven experts are not alone in their interpretation of uncertain data.[1]

Many experts tend to ignore or underestimate uncertainty, and many non-experts do so too. It seems to be a trait of our behavioural DNA. The impacts of such ignorance can be vast – resulting not just in prison sentences and deaths but also being unprepared for unanticipated changes, missing opportunities, chances for improvements and incurring financial losses. And yet there are also examples to the contrary.

One example in this regard is the prediction of a snow storm for the northeast coast of the US and particularly the reaction of New York's mayor, Bill de Blasio, to this prediction. On 26 January 2015, the US National Weather Service (NWS) stated that the region could be hit by a "potentially historic blizzard"

---

1   On 10 November 2014, the convictions were overturned after appeal with the statement that there was "no case to answer".

with up to 90 cm of snow. As a response to this warning, de Blasio braced the city to "prepare for the worst" as the storm could be the worst in the history of New York City. The city shut down, halting parts of its public transport system and road travel – a major operation for a city as vast and densely populated as New York City.

On 27 January, it became clear that the storm was not going to "live up" to the predictions of its historic magnitude. News reports stated that de Blasio had overreacted to the warnings. What had happened? The storm had moved further east than forecast and thus left the city faster than expected. The NWS admitted the high level of uncertainty connected to predicting these types of snow storms. They stated that "rapidly deepening winter storms are very challenging to predict". There was not much they could do to reduce this uncertainty and give more specific and accurate predictions. In fact, their forecast was full of expressions of this uncertainty; they used words such as "potentially". But de Blasio *overestimated* this uncertainty and went for the worst-case predictions. His defence was "My job as a leader is to make decisions and I will always err on the side of safety and caution."

I Think vs You Think

Many decisions in "the real world"[2] rely heavily on our perceptions of the situation. I may not always want to go out for Thai food for dinner but sometimes it might just be the right thing for me, especially when I do not feel like cooking myself. This perception leads me to make a certain choice over another option. When I make this decision together with my husband, the outcome also depends heavily on his perception. If he prefers Thai food for tonight and I do not, we might end up having to make a compromise. Irrespective of what this compromise might be in the end, our decisions are based on our perceptions of the situation and these often differ between people.

Under uncertainty, this perception can take the form of a degree of belief or subjective probability. This degree of belief represents what we think the likelihood is that an uncertain event will happen. For example, we saw in Chapter 2 that people can perceive the likelihood when flipping a coin to be vastly different from 50 per cent. These degrees of belief are often affected by

---

2 This is the term many researchers use for clarifying the difference between simplified decision-making models and the complexity that impacts decision making in our everyday lives. This basically excuses any errors that the predictions from the simplified models might give.

our attitudes. If I think I am able to deal with an uncertain situation, I may follow Randy Komisar's example (remember him from Chapter 4?) and embrace uncertainty in my life and in my career. In other situations our emotions get the better of us and we make snap decisions, preferring one option over the other without being able to clearly articulate why we have come to this determination.

Thus our degrees of belief cannot be judged as to whether they are right or wrong. Sometimes we simply have to accept that we have different opinions, different viewpoints on a situation and a different perception of the uncertainty. In some situations, our beliefs can be judged on their level of realism or how closely connected they are to reality. In many scientific experiments, researchers have used extant uncertainty in the form of (objective) probability values and distributions for this. The outcome of a throw of a coin is 50 per cent and the outcome of a throw of dice is 1 in 6 and so on. In other cases, we can observe what actually happens – say the magnitude of an earthquake or the actual magnitude of a predicted storm.

Systemic Thinking

Our perceptions lead the decisions we make, and our perceptions can fool us or lead us into dilemmas. It is almost as if we have two different minds that tell us to do two different things. And in fact, this is what psychology research tells us we do.

Psychology research suggests that we have two systems of reasoning. These run under various names and for the purpose of this book, let us refer to them as System 1 and System 2. These two systems support fundamentally different ways of how we process information, make sense of the world around us and ultimately how we make decisions.

System 1 applies associative processes where we react intuitively and automatically to situations around us. Think of a moment when you hear a noise such as a friend calling your name and you turn towards the source of that sound. You tend not to consciously think about where you are turning yourself to, you simply do it. Thinking processes using System 1 are pragmatic, intuitive. We base them on our experience and beliefs and thus often come to a conclusion very fast. The thinking process itself is often implicit, meaning that we are typically consciously aware of the outcome (i.e. the decision) but not the thinking process to obtain this outcome. We turn ourselves towards the source of the sound but are not aware of how we came to the conclusion of facing this particular direction.

System 2, in contrast, operates as rule-based and includes deliberate and controlled processes which apply systematic rules. Think back to your time at school when your mathematics teacher asked you to do mental arithmetic. When I was in school, my maths teacher asked the whole class to stand up at the beginning of the lesson and gave us relatively simple maths problems to solve. When you had the correct answer, you would say it out loud and were allowed to sit down. Whatever your opinion may be about this teaching style, it is a good example of making us use System 2. Thinking processes using System 2 are sequential, controllable, demanding and often slow. Thus we tend to be consciously aware of not only the decision outcome – the correct (or sometimes incorrect) solution to the mathematical problem – but also of the process that led us there.

Both of these systems of reasoning often act at the same time – meaning that we process information using System 1 and System 2. This is what Steven Sloman describes in his works on dual-processing theory. Our decision or response to available information is thus determined by two different ways of processing information – associatively using System 1 and rule-based using System 2. Thus most of our decisions are a result of using both automatic heuristics and controlled applications of rules. What do we need the two systems of reasoning for if we have to come to only one decision?

WHAT DO WE NEED THEM FOR?

Decision researchers often make us believe that decisions are best made deliberately, objectively and with some reflection. They often tell us that we decide through deliberate considerations and careful weighing off of the advantages and disadvantages. This would lead us to believe that ideally, decisions under uncertainty should be made using only System 2 – after careful consideration of the available information and applying existing rules and logic of economic preferences. In practice, however, this is usually not the case.

In real-world scenarios, each of the two systems of reasoning affects the outcome of our decision-making processes. System 1 provides us with quick answers, often based on emotional responses. In Chapter 4, we looked at the different emotional responses we can have in situations of uncertainty. The majority of us probably have felt some form of insecurity or fear or even anxiety when facing uncertain situations. Sometimes, however, we can benefit from uncertainty and feel encouraged or even energised by it. These emotional responses are signs of us using our System 1 thinking.

Emotions correspond to consideration of future consequences in decision making. As such, our emotions entail our expectations about the decision outcome, based on a summary of past experience and other heuristics. Emotions often guide our decision making. When we feel happy and optimistic – because of a recent positive endeavour for example – we tend to embrace uncertainty much more readily than when we feel down or depressed.

When we decide without using our emotions, we may end up making fatal errors. In a study participants (with normal brain functions) were compared in their decision-making to participants with damage to the prefrontal cortex. Damage to the prefrontal cortex reduces the ability to experience emotions such as pleasure or discomfort. The researchers let both groups of participants draw from different stacks of cards and obtain a financial gain or loss depending on the drawn card. Their findings were stunning. First, emotional responses seem to let us "guess" which strategy is advantageous. The normal participants chose advantageously. They were able to draw on emotions such as fear of a losing strategy when making their decisions to find the better stack of cards. The participants even engaged in this behaviour before they could know which strategy would yield advantageous gains. In contrast, a lack of emotions seems to let us ignore which strategy is advantageous. Participants with the damaged prefrontalcortex were found to engage in a disadvantageous strategy even after they knew that it would result in financial losses. In other words, they ignored their fear of losing money and continued to draw cards from the "losing" stack. Thus our emotions seem to make a fundamental difference to our decision making under uncertainty.

Problems arise when our emotional reactions to uncertain situations differ from our cognitive evaluations. In other words, our System 1 tells us something different than our System 2. And in these circumstances, our System 1 often wins; it often defines the dominant behaviour.

In our System 1 processes, we use much more than simply the "relevant" information. We use our expectations of the context to make decisions. Imagine for example that you are involved in construction projects across Europe. Two of these construction projects are at a stage where critical progress is dependent on the weather, and your company has hired a meteorological expert. You meet with this person regularly to assess the situation and decide the next actions in your projects. The expert tells you that there is "a slight chance of rain" for London, the place of one of your construction sites. Worried about the negative impact rain could have you decide not to go ahead with the works in London for now. Later on in the day, the expert tells you that there is "a slight chance of rain" for your construction site in Madrid. With little concern about the low chances of rain, you go ahead with the scheduled work for this site. Despite the same (objective) assessments of the uncertainty, our decisions were guided by our individual expectations and knowledge of the context of our forecast.

Thus our decisions under uncertainty vary greatly with the decision context and the given scenarios. One of the key differentiators is the vividness of the descriptions, or more correctly, the vividness of the mental images we have when reading descriptions of scenarios. As such, warnings – health warnings, severe weather warnings or personal risk warnings – are much more effective if they are based on people and anecdotes. Consider for example the difference between the following two scenarios. You may be given statistical information about the side effects of a new type of medical treatment – say for example that it may cause internal bleeding. In comparison this information may be given to you by the spouse of a patient who died because of internal bleeding following the new medical treatment, laying out the events as they happened. Your immediate response may be that you do not wish to suffer like the patient whose spouse's descriptions you have heard, but you may be willing to accept the small likelihood of the side effect based on statistical information.

Emotions also impact our financial decisions. Studying people's willingness to pay for different types of insurance, participants were found to accept larger payments for insurance covering the death "from terrorist attack" to covering death "from all possible causes". Terrorist attacks cause more vivid mental images than "anything" – maybe because of regular coverage on television and other media that provides images we can easily recall when terrorism is mentioned.

Thus System 1 processes affect our consideration of the available information and subsequently our subjective likelihoods of the different possible outcomes of our decision. Our emotions are core to decision making and in practice impact most of the decisions we make – at least to some degree. Most uncertain situations create an immediate emotional response, an anticipatory effect, and we let these emotions guide our further path of decision making.

Discrepancies between System 1 and System 2 reasoning under uncertainty can be helped – albeit not solved. Improvements of our System 2 can reduce the biases we have in our decision making and encourage us to ponder on our reactions and information processing. Thus, the works of Richard Nisbett and his colleagues have shown that people can learn statistical, probabilistic and methodological rule systems and categorisations which in turn can affect their reasoning. This raises the question: why do we not simply use deliberate processes – so System 2 – when making decisions under uncertainty?

DISRUPTING SYSTEM 1

Our System 1 works faster than our System 2. Affective reactions arise more rapidly than basic cognitive evaluations. People can have affective reactions before they even know what they are reacting to. This is especially important in situations of imminent danger when seconds can make a decisive difference. This could be the case in emergency situations such as when we are about to have an accident and our immediate decisions and actions make a difference to its severity.

In various studies, researchers have looked at the impact of disruptions to our automatic information processing and intuitive reasoning. In studies presented by Timothy Wilson and Jonathan Schooler, study participants were asked to disrupt these System 1 processes and analyse and decompose them. This is a method called introspection – letting participants experience a situation and then asking their opinion and memory of this experience. The researchers' aim was to identify why people come to certain conclusions using System 1 – but their findings have an important added significance.

They found that introspection has a disruptive effect when making decisions. When you are asked about your preference for two options – say two different dishes, two pairs of trousers, two restaurants or two holiday destinations – you form these preferences based on System 1 reasoning. When asked why you made this choice, it causes you to interrupt this process and this has significant effects for the outcome. Asked about why they had the observed preferences, the participants came up with certain arguments. When these arguments should have led them to a different set of preferences, they would change their behaviour. In other words, an uninterrupted decision-making process led the participants to one decision and interrupting this process led them to a contradicting decision – simply because they were forced to voice their System 1 reasoning and felt compelled to act in accordance with the stated reasons.

Other research has come to similar conclusions. In other studies, participants were asked to describe why they felt a certain way. Thinking of various reasons that would explain their anger or disappointment, some participants came up with arguments that were discrepant from their initial attitude and then adopted the attitude implied by these reasons. In one study, for example, participants were asked to rate different jams. The participants changed their evaluation when they were required to fill in a questionnaire to rank different characteristics of the jams such as sweetness, bitterness and aroma. The researchers found that with uninterrupted System 1 reasoning, the participants preferred jams that corresponded well with ratings of trained sensory experts, but with interrupted System 1 processing they changed this assessment. This shows not only that introspection is unsuitable to study these processes but also that System 1 processes are very important in our decision making.

In other words, disrupting the System 1 processes can cause discrepancies between attitude and behaviour and thus lead to inconsistencies in our decision making. Thinking about (otherwise) automatic choices may change our evaluations and thus cause people to make less optimal choices. This is particularly the case for decisions containing a large affective component – such as choosing a suitable strawberry jam for your breakfast. We tend to change those decisions we make based on our gut feel rather than those where we evaluate the pros and cons.

Thus we need our System 1 to make decisions. More importantly for this work, we need System 1 to make decisions under uncertainty. We need it to evaluate the available information, make use of our past experience and existing knowledge. Emotions help us make approach-avoidance decisions, cognition helps us make true/false judgements. We use the two systems of reasoning for different situations and for different types of decisions. And sometimes they get in each other's way.

Judgment Under Uncertainty

Despite the importance of System 1 for making good decisions under uncertainty, it also often contradicts the considerations of our System 2. It also often leads to inconsistencies in our decision making in comparison to "rational" theoretical predictions. The reason for this is the heuristics our System 1 follows. It leads us down shortcuts and quick routes to come up with quick answers for decision problems. These heuristics lead to decisions making biases – "anomalies" of our reactions and decisions which cause us to prefer one option that we would not pick if we followed the rules imposed to us by classic decision-making theory. Table 5.1 lists and summarises the decision-making biases described here.

I WON'T STRAY TOO FAR FROM HERE

Once we are given a possible option for a decision, we tend to not go too far away from that option. Researchers call this anchoring. Our judgements of values and beliefs are influenced by such an anchor – a starting point that we have at the time of making a decision. How long do you think the river Elbe is – in total? 1000 km? 10000 km? Imagine you asked this question of your friends and family. You divide them into two groups and give them each one of these two possible values for the length of the Elbe. What would happen? The group that was given the 1000 km anchor would give a much lower estimate than the group given the 10000 km anchor.[3] They will show an anchoring bias.

Most of the time, we are influenced by anchors that are relevant for our decision context. When we estimate the budget for our summer holiday this year, we can base our decision on the amount of money we used last year. Similarly, when I agree to meet with my friends in a bar in town, I can estimate how long it will take me to get there based on previous durations of my journey.

The issue with anchoring bias is that the bias still exists with irrelevant anchors. For example, if you thought about the last four digits of your telephone number before estimating the length of the river Elbe, your estimate would be influenced by this anchor even though you know that it is irrelevant information. The fun of experimental research lies in the possibility of testing different scenarios and research hypotheses. Consequently, the impact of irrelevant anchors has been shown to exist in various decisions: when we estimate prices, probabilities, answer factual knowledge questions and so on. It exists also as non-numerical anchors when we compare the pleasantness of a scent, the heaviness of a weight or the intensity of a shock to something we had experienced previously.

The anchoring bias has had the longest history of the decision-making biases under uncertainty: the first studies were reported in the 1930s. Then it was connected to psychophysics studies which aim at estimating physical characteristics such as length, weight or speed. The researchers observed a contrast effect of anchors. The longer a comparison piece of music was, the shorter the estimate of the target piece of music. The heavier the comparison weight, the lighter was the estimate about the target weight and so on. Because of this length of research on anchoring bias, it has also been linked to some of the decision-making biases described overleaf.

I CAN'T THINK OF ANYTHING ELSE

Recent events bias our decision making. Based on recent observations, we tend to overemphasise how likely these observed events actually are and

---

3   Unless, of course, they know the correct answer: 1094 km.

base our decisions on these overestimations. This has also been called the frequency illusion.

An example is the events following the 1989 earthquake in California. Different geographical regions have a certain probability that they will be hit by an earthquake. This probability is a mean value and does not change when an earthquake has hit. Thus there is no reason to change one's behaviour following a recent event. Despite this, the number of sold policies in California rose significantly after the earthquake in 1989. The reason was that recent events tend to be overemphasised when we make judgements and thus bias our decision making.

I THINK SO, TOO

Often when we are uncertain about a decision we have a gut feeling or a hypothesis. Then we search for information and in this search we focus on information that supports our initial hypothesis. This is called confirmation bias. The confirmation bias states that we tend to seek information that is consistent with our current hypothesis and are unlikely to search for information that is inconsistent with this hypothesis.

An example is the golden rule of first impressions. Imagine you meet someone for the first time – a future colleague, your child's boy or girlfriend. You have agreed a time to meet somewhere, but this person is already late. You are not happy. When they finally arrive, you notice that their shirt is of an odd colour, their shoes are not clean and they have a strange taste in music. Your initial hypothesis – not liking the person because they arrived late – was confirmed by all the subsequent observations you made.

Imagine in contrast that you have heard or read about this person you are about to meet for the first time and are very impressed by them. When you meet them, you notice that they are wearing the brand of trousers that you like, share your political views and like the same food as you do. Your initial hypothesis – you liking them because you respected what you heard or read about them – tainted your observations about this person.

I DON'T KNOW ABOUT THAT!

Similar to confirmation bias, we also tend to avoid information that would contradict our initial hypothesis. We have a clear preference for supportive rather than non-supportive information. Even worse, we often tend to avoid or ignore information that does not conform to our opinion. We deliberately close our eyes to this part of reality. This phenomenon goes under various terms in the literature such as selective consideration, wilful blindness or ignorance, selective exposure and information avoidance. The underlying phenomenon is the same.

We specifically avoid information that is threatening. It may contradict our worldview, threaten our cherished beliefs, a current desired emotion or a desired habituated behaviour. If we were to face the information, we would have to draw some painful conclusions. We would have to accept that our current worldview is limited and our beliefs are wrong. Thus we avoid this information. I don't know what I don't want to know.

IT IS NOT WHAT YOU SAID; IT'S HOW YOU SAID IT!

Our judgements are impacted by the way information is presented to us. The way it is labelled or framed causes us to go down specific mental routes and avoid others. This is called the framing effect or framing bias. The glass can be either half full or half empty and depending on this label we make different judgements.

This decision-making bias has been used by various researchers. Consider the following example. You are trying to decide whether to implement a new method for treating cancer. To make this decision, you do a survey of some experts in the field who you divide into two groups. The first group is told that the treatment method has a 50 per cent success rate; the second group is told that it has a 50 per cent failure rate. Both labels convey the same information but the framing is different. Subsequently, the answers you will get from both groups will be different. The first group is more likely to accept the new treatment method than the second group. What happens when these groups make their judgements?

Consider Figure 5.1. The two groups of experts are given two different labels – a success and a failure label. The failure label raises negative associations – all the things that can go wrong with new treatment methods – while the success label raises positive associations – all the people that may be helped. In their evaluations, the experts are then likely to make some adjustments before stating their decision. These adjustments are too small to counter the effect of the initial label or decision frame.

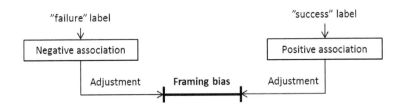

FIGURE 5.1 FRAMING BIAS

The framing bias can be observed in many different decision examples. Framing the outcome of a gamble in terms of gains or losses can lead to different decisions. We tend to be influenced by the manner in which information is presented to us, except when the decision is concerned with a highly personal or moral decision such as cheating or stealing. These are examples where the framing bias could not be proven by researchers.

I WOULD HAVE DONE BETTER

Many historians state that the outbreak of the First World War was evident and unavoidable. The tensions between the European powers at the time were so charged that conflict was inevitable. Yet at the time it came as a surprise to a good many people. We tend to be biased in the safe veil of hindsight.

Hindsight and foresight differ fundamentally – amongst other things in the amount of available information to the observer. In hindsight, we know what happened and this knowledge leads us to believe that this outcome was self-evident. In foresight, we lack this knowledge and thus are not so sure about the likely outcome. Knowing the outcome of a situation has been shown to increase our perceived probability of its occurrence. Knowing that the First World War started on 28 July 1914 means that historians can interpret the events leading up to this date in light of the outcome – namely the start of a global war. With the lack of this knowledge, the events could have resulted in various other outcomes.

This results in the tendency for a decision maker with outcome knowledge to falsely believe that they would have predicted the outcome. The interesting point is that we are unaware of this bias and are thus unlikely to change its impact on our judgements. Our hindsight bias often gets the better of us.

IT'S A BIT LIKE …

Which event would you be more likely to take out travel insurance for: flight disruptions due to terrorist activity or flight disruptions due to any event? If you say the first, then you are in the company of most travellers participating in a study in the early 1990s. What is so strange about this decision? Terrorist activities qualify as "any event" and thus the second option would be much more likely than the first option. Yet many of us judge it more likely that we will be a victim of terrorist activity. This has been named by researchers as the conjunction fallacy. It states that people judge specific conditions to be more likely than a single general condition. Disruption by terrorist activity is more likely than disruption by any event.

This effect is connected to representativeness. People often judge probabilities on the basis of similarity or representativeness. This phenomenon can be observed in many social judgements – when we judge people's traits, their future behaviour or performance. It is linked to the issue of overgeneralisation. We may have made one observation in the past and associate a specific person with this observation. Then we overgeneralise the likelihood of an unrelated judgement.

TABLE 5.1   EXEMPLAR DECISION-MAKING BIASES

Decision-making biases	What it means
Anchoring	An estimate is given too close to an anchor value. This anchor value can be relevant to the estimate, contain irrelevant information or be self-generated by the estimator.
Frequency illusion	Recent events appear more likely that they actually are and we thus overemphasise them in our decision making.
Confirmation	We selectively search for and recollect information that supports our hypothesis or current opinion about an issue. We then make a decision on this biased information because of the amble evidence and support in favour of it.
Selective consideration	We avoid information that contradicts our current belief and opinion, particularly when we perceive this contradicting information to be threatening – to our beliefs, emotions or behaviour. We close our eyes to what would otherwise be obvious.
Framing effect	The manner in which the options or available information are presented to us affects our judgement and decisions. The glass may be half full or half empty.
Hindsight bias	In hindsight, we know what the outcome of a decision-problem is. With this knowledge, we tend to overestimate that we would have made the appropriate decision at the time.
Conjunction fallacy	People judge specific conditions to be more likely than a single general condition and thus bias their decisions toward less probable events.

Why We Judge as We Do

Researchers have speculated for decades now about the possible reasons for the decision-making biases introduced above. Finding and proving the right answer is not that easy in psychology because we can only observe and measure the outcome – i.e. the decision-making bias – and not the process that led to it. Thus various explanations have been put forward and developed by the community. The explanation that has received most approval has been the activation mechanism.

The activation mechanism is based on the assumption that we can only consider a limited amount of information when making judgements and decisions. We recall information from our memory and experience or search for external information. In any case, only "activated" information is considered in the process. It is this activated information that biases our decisions. When we are given an anchor – a starting point for our judgement – we base our decision-making process on information that is activated by this anchor. When we already have a hypothesis for our judgement, we activate the information that confirms this hypothesis and "deactivate" information that does not. When we are given a positively framed statement, we activate positive information to make our judgement. And so on.

That means that the activation mechanism can explain most of the decision-making biases mentioned above. The different biases rely on the fundamental process that specific information is more or less available. When we make decisions, judgements or evaluations, we do not retrieve the judgement from memory but process it online. We think about the task – that is, we compute the available input and other relevant (and possibly irrelevant) information and come up with an answer to the problem. Our evaluation of an issue depends on our ability to retrieve evidence for or against it. We evaluate something as more likely the more examples we can come up with in favour of the issue and the easier it is to come up with these examples. We evaluate something as less likely the more counter-examples we can think of and the easier these counter-examples come to mind.

Thus in different situations, when the given input differs due to different framing of the problem, different anchors and so on, we may come to different decisions. Receiving an anchor for our decision – whether relevant or irrelevant – makes the information that is consistent with the anchor more available. We can use "anchoring as activation".

Translating this logic into the systemic thinking described above, we can say that both Systems 1 and 2 are involved in making judgements and decisions.

System 2 works on with the information that is retrieved from memory but the retrieval process is completed by System 1. The different causes of decision biases mentioned above – anchor, recent events, framing, hindsight and so on – bias the retrieval process. They steer System 1 towards specific information and make this information more available for System 2.

Adjusting the retrieved information for relevance and usefulness in the given context is then the task of System 2. However, this task is effortful. Researchers have shown that when our System 2 is occupied and our mental resources depleted, System 2 makes less adjustments to retrieved information. In the specific studies, the researchers asked the participants to memorise some digits[4] or to drink alcohol. The insufficient adjustment in these situations is thus a failure of System 2 because it is already engaged, weak or lazy.

Thus the more our System 1 takes over, the more susceptible we are to these decision biases. In these situations, we tend to just "go with the flow" rather than evaluate the information and make an informed choice. This is particularly the case in situations when we are very emotional – happy or sad, when we feel powerful or when we are knowledgeable novices rather than true experts. Similarly, people who score high on a scale of faith in intuition tend to be guided more by System 1 and are thus prone to decision biases.

---

4   This is a typical experimental task when we want to study how much effort a certain thinking task involves because memorising digits requires our concentration and focus, taking this concentration away from the thinking task. The experimental findings thus tend to be more realistic.

CHAPTER 6

Acting on Uncertainty

In 1990, Iben Browning predicted a 50 per cent chance that a severe earthquake would occur in the New Madrid fault[1] in the USA around 2 and 3 December 1990. He has in fact gained notoriety for this prediction. It was widely reported in the national media and as you can imagine caused a huge amount of worry among the residents of the Mississippi Valley. The problem with this prediction was that it was solely based on opinion and sensationalism. Iben Browning was a climatologist and retired business consultant. He had no training in geology nor any proof for his prediction.

Seismologists were busy with denying the prediction as there was no reason to believe that (a) an earthquake would hit the area on that day (it is in fact practically impossible to predict the exact timing of an earthquake) and (b) that there would be an earthquake of severe strength. Their predictions were in fact closer to a 2 per cent chance – a huge difference to Browning's estimation of 50 per cent. They even held a special conference to discredit Browning's claims, yet once the word was out, there was little they could do to refute the predictions. In fact, 2 and 3 December 1990 went by without any tremors.

But the uncertainty of the prediction caused various responses from the residents. The sales of earthquake insurances in the area rocketed. The number of earthquake insurances taken more than tripled in 1990, and the policy sales in October 1990 alone were higher than in the whole of 1989. While these observations come from the fear of the population and their felt need to protect their property against earthquake damage, the story teaches another important lesson about uncertainty.

We are willing to take actions – sometimes drastic actions – when we are faced with uncertainty. Uncertainty does not just impact the way we feel and decide, but even the way we act in different situations. These actions are impacted by the way we make sense out of the possibility of future events and outcomes. We are likely and willing to think counterfactually about undesired outcomes. Browning's predictions were not based on any evidence, yet many

---

1 The New Madrid fault is a 240 km-long fault stretching through five states within the USA from Illinois in the north to Arkansas in the south, and is situated within the Mississippi Valley in this area.

people believed him. We often act on uncertainty based on mixed motives. These mixed motives are what we will explore in this chapter.

Taking Action

Our experiences and decisions under uncertainty – including the biases and misinterpretations that go along with them – are the basis of many of our actions. They even inspire us to act in certain ways. Researchers around Baruch Fischhoff found that participants of their experimental studies were not only giving them statements of overconfidence but were also willing to act on these (mis-)perceptions. The researchers asked the participants if they would bet on their assessments – including the possibility to lose their money. This shows that in reality, overconfidence can be a costly endeavour – quite literally in this specific experiment.

This thinking has found its way into many theories in the social sciences. Our perception of the uncertainty in a situation impacts the actions we take, and in most cases, these actions are motivated by our drive to reduce uncertainty – at least this is what current theory is trying to tell us. There are different ways to reduce uncertainty. Given that uncertainty is a lack of knowledge, the most straightforward approach is to increase our knowledge about the situation, its influences and possible outcomes. For example, if I am really concerned about what to wear tomorrow, I would check the weather forecast to reduce my uncertainty and increase my knowledge about the most likely future states.

Maybe Someone Else Knows

Uncertainty often makes us want to run away from it, stop our exposure to it and retreat to a safe haven. Uncertainty is fine as long as it doesn't affect us. We have an automatic drive that wants to have answers and hard data; we don't want uncertainty or vagueness. Uncertainty reduction seems the natural and first reaction. Thus uncertainty is the starting point of many of our actions.

Our first action may be to seek information. This means to collect, record, or review any new information that may be available about the situation we are in. It can be any relevant – and sometimes irrelevant – information. Imagine, for example, that you try to choose a restaurant in a city you do not know – either because you just moved there or are on holiday. There are various different options available and you are uncertain which one to choose. You have never been to any of these restaurants and have no idea whether you will like their food, if the staff is friendly and if the ambience suits you. What will you do to make your decision?

In such situations, you may start with looking at the menus of the available restaurants; check the price ranges, available food options and so on. Look for reviews online or if you are there, check the places out in person. You may also try to see which of the places is fullest – other people are probably less uncertain than you and thus know which restaurant is the better place. In other words, you seek for available information – anything that reduces your uncertainty and helps you make your decision.

This is also what scientists try to tell us we (should) do. The first call of action when facing uncertainty is to reduce it by seeking new information. The sources of this information can be varied and differ in their ability to facilitate understanding and shared meaning. Imagine for example the difference it makes for you to be given a number or talk to a person face-to-face. The difference for evaluating a restaurant, for example. On different webpages, you may find that restaurants get different scores – 4 out of 5 stars, 8.8 out of 10 possible points and so on. You can compare the values of different restaurants and choose the one with the highest score. Imagine one of your friends has been to one of the restaurants and tells you about their visit – how the waiter joked with them about the weather, offered them a special dish that was not on the menu and replaced a cold dish. Your friend's explanations are difficult to summarise in a number but it gives you a good impression of the qualities of the restaurants.

In the 1980s, researchers around Richard Daft and Robert Lengel tried to position the different sources of information we have available in our professional lives on a scale. They named this scale "media richness". A rich medium can help you gain insight and rapid understanding. You get instant feedback when you ask a question and can thus correct misunderstandings. Rich media also give you various cues. In face-to-face meetings, you will not only receive *what* is being said but also *how* it is said. You can interpret the speaker's voice and intonation, body language, graphic gestures. One example is that conveying sarcasm via email usually does not reach the other end, but in person it often does. The reason for this that in person we can give more cues – intonation, raised eyebrows and so on – so the other person can understand that we are being sarcastic.

The media richness scale was composed before the Internet was a common part of our lives and changed our communications as fundamentally as it has.

It has to be adapted a little to capture the work lives we live now, but the basic principle is still applicable. In Figure 6.1 you can see the media richness scale with some examples. The higher the richness of the medium we seek our information from, the higher the potential for reducing our uncertainty.

When we seek new information, we increase our own knowledge. Researchers would say we process the information through interpretation, reasoning, drawing inferences or learning, and thus include it into our knowledge system. In other words, we try to "understand" the information we face. Rich media helps us do this more easily than less rich media. When we talk to someone face-to-face or on the phone, we can get immediate feedback on our questions and comments. The other person can clarify misunderstandings or wrong assumptions we may have. When you see numerical information or entries in wikis, you cannot clarify the underlying assumptions or find out how applicable this information is to your problem.

When we acquire new information, it increases our knowledge, confirms or disconfirms prior beliefs and adds meaning because it provides explanations for different available options or observations we make. It helps us make sense of the world around us and guide our future decisions and actions.

Information-seeking and processing is one way of acting on uncertainty by trying to reduce it. But this is not the only reaction we have to uncertainty. A

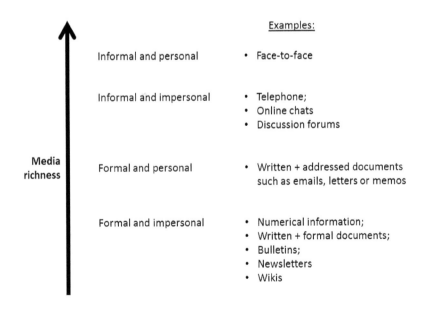

FIGURE 6.1 MEDIA RICHNESS SCALE

lot of the time, we simply choose to ignore uncertainty – because we learnt to live with it or we don't see it relevant for our endeavours. We can cross the road, have a shower and drive in our cars without worrying about the unknown. We learnt to live with some uncertainty without acknowledging it – we choose to ignore it.

This is None of My Business

We are not always motivated to reduce uncertainty. An example is a situation when we meet a new person – someone we have never met before and did not know anything about – for the first time. We do not always try to reduce our uncertainty about new people we meet. Think of some people you have met in a bar for example, or the waiter in a restaurant. Often we do not engage them in personal conversations. We will feel the need to reduce our uncertainty about another person only under specific when this person acts in a deviant fashion, they provide us with rewards or we anticipate seeing them again in the future. If none of these factors hold, we feel no need to reduce the uncertainty and rather ignore it.

Researchers have given much less attention to uncertainty avoidance – or rather to the deliberate avoidance of information that we do not want to have. One of the reasons for this could be that researchers by definition want to develop new knowledge and thus try to collect as much information as they can. Many researchers I know devour one book after the other. But in reality, many of us deliberately close our eyes to some of the uncertainty we perceive and experience and avoid collecting new information about it.

Remember Rokeach? Milton Rokeach was a social psychologist and we talked about him in Chapter 4, Accepting uncertainty. He differentiated types of people based on their ability to deal with uncertainty and incorporate unexpected or unanticipated information into their attitudes and actions. Information avoidance can thus be attributed to more closed-minded people or people whose belief system is oriented towards familiar and predictable events. He called these "psychoanalytic types" of people. He contrasted these from "gestalt types" of people who are open minded and oriented towards new beliefs and information.

In practice however, this behaviour of seeking or avoiding new information is very dependent on situations. We avoid new information in situations when certainty does not allow us to take any better actions. Or at least we feel and fear it does not. So it does not come as much of a surprise that much of the research describing information avoidance is linked to cancer research. People who perceive a cancer diagnosis as being practically given a death sentence will deliberately avoid information about cancer in general. In contrast, people who explicitly search for information on cancer typically have some form of history with it – maybe because a family member or close friend had it.

Information avoidance is closely linked to our System 1 of thinking, particularly to emotions of fear and anxiety. We are afraid of what this new information might tell us. It threatens us and our current belief system. Cancer has been an area that ticks all the boxes: expecting the diagnosis to be a death sentence, perceptions of the ability to treat it and even the uncertainty of the diagnosis itself. People with these attitudes towards cancer in general are more likely to avoid any new information regarding cancer, even of lifestyle choices that could drastically reduce the likelihood of getting cancer.

When we have these attitudes towards a topic – attitudes of great fear or even anxiety – we short-circuit our usual information-seeking activities, maybe because we fear that any information we would find could only be bad, devastating even. So we simply avoid being confronted with this new information at all.

In many situations, we have to choose to follow certain routes and by proxy avoid others. This is because we make a lot of our daily decisions and actions under constraints of time and effort, so we have to choose not to do some things. For example, at school I had to decide which language to learn in class – I could only choose one option between French, Spanish and Russian. Choosing one meant that I could not do the other two. The same goes for many other decisions – from choosing a meal in a restaurant to choosing treatment methods when we or someone in our family becomes ill.

We thus regularly avoid information by turning our attention into another direction in our lives. By default we avoid letting some information into our lives – because we lack the time, energy or attention. And it can become a habit to shut out the "inconvenient" information that challenges our beliefs and our habits. We love to do things the way we have always done them. But sometimes it can be beneficial to lean into uncertainty and use it to create something new. We can use uncertainty as a springboard for creativity, creation and exploration.

Let Us Use the Uncertainty!

Uncertainty is wondrous, and certainty, were it to be real, would be moral death. If we were certain of the future, there could be no moral compulsion to do anything. We would be free to indulge every passion and pursue every egoism, since all actions fall within the certainty that has been ordained. If everything is uncertain, then the future is open to creativity, not merely human creativity but the creativity of all nature. It is open to possibility, and therefore to a better world.

Immanuel Wallerstein in *"Uncertainty and Creativity"*, 1997

Uncertainty can be a strong source of positive and creative action. Uncertainty gives possibility and therefore offers hope for a better world as we create it. Uncertainty means that tomorrow can look completely different from today and we have the power and responsibility to shape this tomorrow. Those that can leverage the uncertainty and use it for creating something new and better will be the ones who succeed and shape the future. Those that shun uncertainty will be the ones who will follow the creators.

Researchers have highlighted the positive power of uncertainty but seem to have failed to understand the implications of this. There is little research that looks at the empowering role of uncertainty in the actions we take and even less research focuses on the role of uncertainty in creativity and creation. Existing links between uncertainty and the facilitating role it can play are few and far between.

Uncertainty is the enabler of building and having trust. Think of someone you trust – your spouse, a friend, brother or sister or a parent. Trust is essentially a leap of faith into that person's present and future actions. We trust our family and friends not to betray or deceive us. And we can only have this trust because there is the possibility that they might. There is uncertainty about the future actions they might take and an action that would damage us is a possibility – even if remote. Uncertainty enables trust and is even the prerequisite for us trusting other people.

Similarly, uncertainty enables us to do many other things. It can be a liberating force. It is the facilitator of innovation, of collaborations and creation, and it enables us to build a better future. It creates the possibility for opportunities and only if we keep our eyes and mind open will we be able to see and grasp these opportunities. Many of us have understood this and live by it every day. Yet research is limping behind in this area and much work needs to be done in this field.

PART II
ORGANISATIONS AND UNCERTAINTY

We can describe organisations as systems of people, where each person performs a specific task. Organisations also contain technologies and processes, have to deal with suppliers and customers and stay ahead of competitors. For the purposes of this second part of this book, we look at organisations as a collection of people. The activities and decisions that managers, administrators, engineers, technicians and so on take impact the success of organisations as a whole. This enables us to translate some of the points we discussed in the first part of this book – people and uncertainty – into the context of our work lives in organisations.

An organisation can take various forms. It can be a company that tries to generate profits and stay ahead of competition. It can be a non-profit organisation and work for charity. It can exist around a part-time club such as volleyball or sailing. The important characteristic of organisations for this book is that they consist of people and these people fulfil different roles. Organisations are also surrounded by uncertainty and have various possibilities of dealing with it – similar to individuals. In Part II, we will explore how uncertainty can look for organisations and what organisations' possibilities of dealing with it are.

Thus this part of the book underlies two central assumptions. First, the behaviour of individuals influences the behaviour of organisations. When we interact with colleagues, superiors and mentees at our workplace, the way we engage with them creates a central part of the organisational culture. The amount of respect, personal liking, intellect and sensitivity we give and are given in these interactions affect the work environment. The mental models of the individual employees, their attention and cognition impact the organisation as a whole. They affect how we interact with each other and subsequently organisational behaviour. Thus, individual behaviour patterns can be translated up to organisational patterns.

The second assumption is that organisations affect our individual behaviour. We spend much of our lives at work. Depending on the job, industry sector, work culture and company, this may well be the majority of our daily lives. Thus the working culture and social interactions we see and experience at our work institutions affect our personal behaviours. The extent to which we feel our work is valued can impact our overall level of happiness, our mood, and our appreciation for colleagues and friends. Organisational behaviour also has a considerable impact on our personal behaviours and determines some interesting and important patterns. Organisations can be analysed on an individual level to investigate, for example, how we socialise with each other, how we progress in our careers, or how we decide or act within the context of the organisation we work in.

The insights from Part I are relevant in the context of organisations and we will analyse their applicability in Part II of this book. Many concepts that are relevant on the individual level are also important in organisations: just think of fairness, motivation, social interactions or respect. As much as these concepts influence our actions in our private lives, and similarly theory in the field of social interactions, they are also applicable for our professional lives in describing the relationships we have with our peers, supervisors and supervisees.

In this part, we will look at the following four issues:

- Organisations and uncertainty types
- Uncertainty and time
- Organisational decision making
- Organisational actions.

CHAPTER 7
Organisations and Uncertainty Types

Starting in December 2010, the Arab Spring was a wave of political and social instability accompanied by protests that swept through Arab countries in North Africa and the Middle East. Many countries such as Tunisia, Egypt, Libya and Yemen had their governments and rulers overthrown. Public squares and whole cities were often unpassable for weeks or months due to violent and non-violent protests. The deaths of tens of thousands of people have been tied to the Arab Spring, and many countries resembled a war zone for months. In others, the general public was placed on curfew and supplies of gas and electricity became a serious problem in these areas.

Subsequently, organisations struggled. Many had to close their businesses because they could not continue production, lacking supplies and staff. Many people lost their jobs. Economic and political instability took their toll on the countries, their governments and the general public as well as the organisations operating in this area. Organisations face various challenges like these, albeit usually not to the same extremes as during and following the Arab Spring. Extreme external events are reported regularly: examples include the nuclear meltdown of Fukushima in 2011 and the Hong Kong protests in 2014, each causing substantial challenges and disruptions for organisations and whole supply chains.

Crises like the Arab Spring cause high levels of uncertainty for organisations with regard to the future of their business, the decisions and actions they should take in these situations and the possibilities of achieving their goals. Thus organisations have increasingly to be able to deal with uncertainty. The uncertainty comes from various directions and unprepared or unresponsive organisations are usually left behind. In this chapter, we take a look at what these uncertainties can be and how they may affect organisations.

The Complexity of Organisations

Organisations consist of different people who fulfil various roles and in combination make up the strategic positioning of the organisation. There are multiple departments that provide inputs and outputs for each other and jointly deliver value to the customer. There is often an administration, production, human resources, marketing, research and development. For example, a school has not only teachers for the different subjects students need to learn but also a secretariat, headmaster and caretakers. It interacts with other schools in the city and the local community and reports to the regional education ministry as well as parents.

In short, organisations are complex. They often fulfil multiple functions and are embedded in a specific context that is impacted by economic, political, social and technological interactions with other organisations and individuals. An organisation can fulfil multiple roles – it is an employer for staff, a provider or supplier for customers, a competitor in their market segment and a customer for their suppliers.

Thus the uncertainty organisations are exposed to is also complex. For organisations – as well as for individuals – uncertainty is a multilayered concept because it can mean different things to different actors. The difference is that for organisations we can differentiate types of uncertainty. The different uncertainty types have their own characteristics which means that organisations perceive and need to respond to them differently.

You can visualise this as a similarity to cooking. Imagine you want to prepare a specific dish, say macaroni cheese. You have different ingredients for this and each ingredient needs specific preparation before it can be combined to form your dinner of macaroni cheese. The pasta needs to be boiled in water, the cheese grated and the oven preheated.

There are similarities between what you need to do when preparing macaroni cheese to what organisations do when they deal with uncertainty. The different uncertainty types are the ingredients – macaroni and cheese – and the organisational responses to these different uncertainty types are the different cooking methods – boiling in water and grating. Figure 7.1 symbolises the similarities between cooking macaroni cheese and organisations' reactions to uncertainty.

We can take this analogy even further by increasing the complexity of the dish, say a Sunday roast or a curry – or conversely the complexity of the organisation. Then you have even more ingredients with even more varied methods of preparing and combining them to make the final dish. The

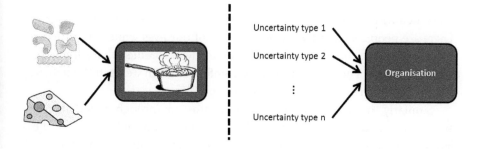

FIGURE 7.1 UNCERTAINTY TYPES AND ORGANISATIONS

organisation's complexity is higher and subsequently the uncertainty it has to deal with is also higher. In an organisational context, uncertainty becomes a more varied and complex concept because of the complexity of organisations.

Uncertainty Types

For organisations uncertainty can arise from different sources. Going back to our cooking analogy, you can think of the different places you will need to get your ingredients from: the vegetables from the local greengrocer or farmer's market, the meat from the butcher, the sides from the supermarket and so on. You may even grow some of the ingredients yourself. Your cooking ingredients come from different sources and these are comparable to an organisation's sources of different uncertainty types.

Uncertainty types can arise from different parts within and surrounding an organisation: Figure 7.2 attempts to depict that. Some of the uncertainty can arise from within the organisation and a lack of knowledge regarding processes or tasks it needs to fulfil. For example, a member of staff who has worked for the organisation has left (to go into retirement or to move into a different job). With this person a lot of tacit knowledge that cannot be easily stored also left the company. Once they left, the organisation faced the lack of this knowledge or uncertainty. This is organisational uncertainty as it arises from within the organisation.

Organisations usually build relationships with other organisations. These can be customers, suppliers, governmental bodies or other collaborators. These interorganisational relationships are a bit like the relationships we build in our lives. Some people we call friends, some are close friends, sometimes we lose touch with some of our friends and sometimes we build new relationships. There are people we trust with close secrets of our lives while with others we keep our distance. In any case, it is difficult to always predict what a friend may do in the future. They may surprise us, comfort us when we need them, betray our trust in them or simply disappear from our lives.

Similarly, interorganisational relationships go through different cycles as they are established, maintained and come to an end. Some of these interorganisational relationships are closer than others. On this level, it is also difficult to predict what a partner may do in the future. They may provide essential and useful knowledge for innovation tasks, they may use the knowledge provided by the focal organisation to their advantage (and the focal organisation's disadvantage), they may release sensitive information to competitors or other third parties. Relationships always have some level of uncertainty attached to them. This is relational uncertainty as it arises from the existence of a relationship with other organisations.

Finally, the organisation exists within its context: the industrial sector, the specific market environment, suppliers, customers and so on. Some of these environments change relatively quickly. Just think of the computer hardware industry and the speed with which processors, storage size and speed evolve. Or the mobile phone industry that is impacted not only by the available hardware

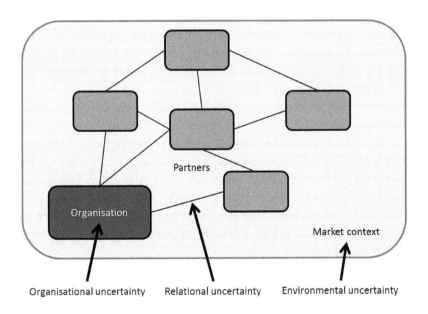

FIGURE 7.2 ORGANISATIONAL, RELATIONAL AND ENVIRONMENTAL UNCERTAINTY

but also the fashion choices of users. In contrast, sectors such as the cement industry have not changed their processes and technologies fundamentally for the last 30 or so years. Thus the environments of organisations can differ drastically and create different incentives to continuously innovate and define a competitive advantage. This gives rise to environmental uncertainty as it arises from the organisation's context or environment.

Organisational Uncertainty

Organisational uncertainty comes from within the organisation, which may lack the knowledge and capability to perform a certain task. Think of this as comparable to when you are trying to do something new, something you have not done before, such as reading a book in a foreign language, building a book shelf for your house, having children or planting a tree. If you have not done something before you can read about it, ask other people, watch online tutorials and so on, but ultimately you will be left with some uncertainty with regard to how to do it. What will happen if you do step 3 before step 2 or if you change some of the steps entirely? The uncertainty you face in these situations is similar to that which organisations face.

However, for organisations things are a little more nuanced. The organisational uncertainty can come from, for example, the loss of the tacit knowledge of a member of staff who retired or left the company. This person knew exactly how their job was done best – what outputs needed to be delivered on time, who they could talk to for specific problems and solutions, where shortcuts could be taken – and once they leave, no one possesses this knowledge any more. The organisation has lost knowledge regarding tasks it has done before.

It may also arise from the different people who are supposed to work in teams towards a joint goal – think for example of teams involved in new product development or a team working on an installation project for a client. These individuals may perceive their team's goal differently – one of them may think that the aim is to deliver an output as quickly as possible, another one might want to come up with the perfect solution and a third person may be worried about the cash flow. They each perceive their goal differently. This creates organisational uncertainty because the differences can cause tensions in the team's activities.

Finally, organisational uncertainty can arise when the organisation engages in new tasks. For example, a company may want to engage with a new client, expand their production to a new country or engage in strategic reorientation of the whole business. Changing things by default involves some uncertainty because plans usually do not work out the way they look on paper. The performance may be difficult to predict and the organisation's capability to achieve the plan is yet to be proven.

WORKING IN PROJECTS

Many organisations work in projects. Developing new products, opening a new branch, merging two departments or implementing new software, these activities are usually completed via projects. Projects are time-constraint types of "mini-organisations" within the organisation. A number of people with the relevant skills from inside and outside of the organisation are grouped together for a set period of time to work on the project and complete the planned outcomes. The key part is that projects exist only for a limited period of time. They are designed to disintegrate as soon as they have served their original purpose.

Imagine you would like to read that book in a foreign language – pick any language for this purpose. You may have learned this language at school but have not used it all that much since then. Or you may not know that language at all before you attempt this project. In any case, you try to achieve your goal and start with learning or freshening up your language skills. You go to a language course, follow an app on your phone, become part of a local community that speaks and trains this language or engage in online chats. This is your project team – they help you achieve your goal.

However, there is also uncertainty in projects. This is project uncertainty and it refers to the uncertainty surrounding the goals, objectives and scope of your project. How difficult is the book you want to read supposed to be? You may achieve your goal of reading a book in a foreign language much faster if you consider children's books or fairy tales rather than books from esteemed classic authors. How long or short should the book be? How much of the plot do you wish to understand to have achieved your goal? Your project goal may be very fuzzy in the beginning but become clearer as you move towards it and define in more detail exactly what you want to achieve.

Project uncertainty is different from organisational uncertainty because it concerns the project, which in turn can involve resources from within and outside of the organisation. A project team may include consultants, clients, suppliers and other partners from outside of the organisation. Project uncertainty is thus distinct from organisational uncertainty. Not all organisations face and have to deal with project uncertainty. Naturally, only those organisations that engage in project work and structure their tasks in and around projects will face project uncertainty, but not all organisations do that.

WORKING IN CONTRACTS

Some organisations may work predominantly in contracts or contractual arrangements. This differs from project work in many ways. Contracts can usually be renewed if both (or all) partners agree to it. Thus, contractual arrangements have less of a time constraint. They are usually agreed for a specific period of time but have a more operational character and do not dissolve as soon as a specific goal is achieved. Instead they exist to support the ongoing operations of an organisation.

Think of your electricity provider. You have at some point signed a contract with them that specifies a payment scheme and rates and estimates your annual use. Once the contract is in place you can use the company's services and are billed for them on a monthly or annual basis. After the contract period, the agreement may automatically be renewed unless you cancel it beforehand. The contractual arrangement you have with your electricity provider does not have a specific end goal after which your agreement ends. It has an operational character for you. It supports you in living and feeling comfortable in your home. You will probably only end your contract once a better option comes along.

This is similar for organisations. They thus face organisational uncertainty on a regular and continuous basis. In some of the research I have done, I worked closely with what researchers call servitized manufacturing companies. These are companies that traditionally produced and manufactured products and equipment. For many reasons, these companies then started providing services for their products and equipment, to help their customers maintain them and keep them in good shape: a strategy a little bit like an extended guarantee. For example, when you buy a car, you get services and inspections for the following years. Your car dealer does not just sell you the car; they sell you the subsequent services as well to make your life a bit easier. This is what servitized manufacturers do. Companies such as Siemens, Grundfos, Rolls-Royce and FLSmidth use this strategy.

When changing the organisation strategy so fundamentally, from providing products to providing services, these companies face high levels of organisational uncertainty. The fundamental processes of providing services are very different from selling products or equipment. How many times do you see the dealer of your car before you buy it? Once or a few times? Usually, once you have bought the car, you stop interacting with the dealer. How often do you go to the garage with your car? Once a year for the MOT or every few years? Every time you have a problem or breakdown of your car? You interact with a service provider on a more regular basis than with a dealer.

On the flip side of the coin this means that the provider needs to be able to accommodate these regular service visits as opposed to the one-off sales. Servitized manufacturers have to change the dynamics of how they work, the staff who do the work for them and their qualifications, the locations of their facilities and so on. Their staff need to be able to deliver service quality, deal with customer requests and give their customers the relevant information rather than produce the products in most efficient and optimised way possible. Subsequently, the companies may need branches that are geographically close to their customers rather than close to providers and cheap labour. There is much organisational uncertainty involved in a fundamental change of organisation strategy such as becoming a servitized manufacturing company.

Relational Uncertainty

Servitized manufacturers also face relational uncertainty. The relationships they start building with their customers can be compared to the relationships we build in our lives. We get to know someone, build trust with them and maybe start a friendship. At some point we might live our lives apart, start having different interests and the relationship comes to an end. Interorganisational relationships share some similarities with this description, especially the relationships that servitized manufacturers have with their customers.

Services need by default the input of both provider and customer. Before your car can be repaired, you need to bring it to the local garage and explain to them what the symptoms of your problem are. The garage can then start investigating what the source of the problem may be and how to repair it. Both of these things are necessary for the service: you bring the car in and the garage personnel investigate and repair the problem. If one of these parts is missing, the service can not be performed. In other words, services by necessity contain a relationship between provider and customer.

Any relationship contains some relational uncertainty. We can never be 100 per cent sure about our partner's future actions – in most cases they might even not know these themselves. This inability to predict the partner's future behaviour and the level of cooperation they will offer us is relational uncertainty. The garage may be very cooperative with you and hand a functioning car back to you in 24 hours. Or they may not prioritise your service and take several weeks to make any repairs. The level of cooperation the garage gives you is uncertain and this uncertainty is relational.

For servitized manufacturers, relational uncertainty can be a considerable influence on their business. Providing services to business customers usually means that the provider comes to the customer to maintain and repair their equipment: the garage is coming to you rather than the other way around. This requires a lot of coordination and communication between the organisations. The provider's service engineers cannot simply turn up when they want; they need to fit the service visits into the schedule of their customers. If the mechanics came to you to maintain your car, they would need to check with you to ascertain when it is that you do not need your car and when you are at home etc. You may have a different schedule every week as you work shifts and change between night and day shifts, or there may be a special event in one week as your daughter or son has a special birthday and so on. All these things provide possible obstacles for coordinating the service business and create relational uncertainty.

This uncertainty is increased when the relationship spans national, language and cultural barriers. The world is becoming smaller through globalisation – or flat, as Thomas Friedman (2005) would say. This means that geographical distances do hinder collaborations and business relationships any more. Companies operate around the globe, be it in Europe, North or South America or Asia. Products and parts are sourced and shipped around the globe. So are many services. This means that organisations have to work with partners whose customs and habits they do not know.

Imagine for example you go to East Asia – either on holiday or to work there. You may not speak the language or speak it only brokenly. You are thus not able to interpret when someone local makes a joke or is being polite. You may not know the local customs or how things are done. What legal procedures do you need to consider, what gestures or mimics are impolite or expected of you? All these things differ between countries, languages and cultural zones. Habits and customs differ between and within Europe, Asia, Africa, North and South America. This makes it even harder to predict your friends' or partners' future behaviours or even to know what to expect.

This elevated level of relational uncertainty also applies on an organisational level. Companies that collaborate with organisations around the globe need to get to know the local ways of doing things. What is expected before business deals are made? What behaviours are deal breakers? How do you see eye-to-eye with each other? These questions are becoming increasingly important as international business links increase and relational uncertainty is of increasing importance to the success of these partnerships.

Environmental Uncertainty

The final uncertainty type we will look at in this chapter is environmental uncertainty – that arising from the organisation's context and market environment. Researchers have focused on this uncertainty types because market turbulences can be observed and followed and often hit hard. Think of the impacts that the 2008–2009 global financial crisis caused for many banks and businesses around the globe. Consider the disruptions that the 2011 tsunami and nuclear disaster in Japan caused for many supply chains. Environmental uncertainty is an important consideration for organisations because they have typically no control over it and often can not foresee these turbulences and disasters.

Environmental uncertainty is particularly linked to the dynamics in the organisation's external context. The more dynamic the market, the higher the level of environmental uncertainty. Consider the markets for computer hardware or mobile phones. These are very dynamic markets and move at a rapid pace. In a year's time their products will look very different from those available now. This makes it virtually impossible to make any predictions for 5, 10 or even 20 years hence. In comparison, slow-moving markets such as the fast-food industry or cement production technology are much easier to predict. These are less dynamic because technologies, processes and markets have not changed fundamentally over recent decades.

Every organisation has to deal with environmental uncertainty on some level and to some degree. It can be related to regular and relatively foreseeable events. For example, many companies struggle with the timing, quantity and quality of deliveries from their suppliers. Others may worry over the demand for their products and services because they wish to plan distribution of the appropriate amount of resources. Variations in supply and demand can cause big problems in production and organisational processes, even if they may be foreseeable.

Then there are other, less foreseeable events, for example the disruptions caused by the destruction and nuclear meltdown in Fukushima in 2011. Others include the student protests in Hong Kong in 2014 that paralysed the whole area for months and disrupted businesses. A further example is the Arab Spring, a wave of political turmoil and unrest that swept through various MENA (Middle East and North Africa) countries with in part devastating effects for local and international organisations operating in the area. These events are beyond the control of the organisations that are affected by them, often cannot be foreseen and can have substantial effects for organisations. Trying to keep operations going under these challenging circumstances requires substantial investment and effort on the part of these organisations.

CHAPTER 8

Uncertainty and Time

What was the weather like in your home town on 21 February 1996? Unless this was a special date for you – a special birthday or even your wedding day – you are unlikely to remember. It may have been a beautiful day and you might have lots of photos with a blue sky and sunshine. Or it may have been a windy and even snowy winter day where the only thing you did was wrap yourself in a blanket in a warm place and read a book or watch TV.

Why would you want to know about the weather on a certain day in a specific place in the past? If the day was a special day for you, it may have some significant relevance for your personal life. The weather also has some significance in determining guilt in our legal systems. Rain and wind can determine the consistency of the ground in woods, parks and so on which in turn can provide proof for whether a person was in a specific place at a given time. So the historic weather situation can be crucial information in determining whether someone is guilty or not of an accused crime.

This is why institutes such as the US Weather Service receive considerable income from selling old weather reports. Their target customers are lawyers who are involved in those cases where the weather can make a difference to the evidence of their client. However, information about the past does not seem to be as readily available. In other words, we can be uncertain about the past even though we have experienced it and so should have the relevant knowledge about it.

With all the previous theory we have discussed in this book, you may have a good idea about the reasons for this observation. Why do we forget some pieces of information while we retain others? The link I am making in this chapter is between uncertainty and time. How does uncertainty develop over time? And how is it linked to our future, present and past?

The Issue of Time

Uncertainty and time are related. Uncertainty can resolve itself as time moves on. The uncertainty we have about a future event, such as tomorrow's weather or the outcome of a throw of dice, disappears when the time has come – when we can see what the weather actually is and which number the throw of dice has given us. So uncertainty fluctuates over time and is related to the progression of time.

But uncertainty is not only related to the future – we can also be uncertain about the past and the present. In his article reflecting on the global financial crisis, Douglas Board writes:

> recent and current economic developments are making it more than usually clear that executives of large corporations and their management consultants, as well as politicians and their advisors, are far from sure of what has been happening and they simply do not know what is now happening, let alone what will happen in the future as a consequence of actions they are taking. (2010, p. 274)

In this excerpt, he highlights that we can be uncertain as to our past and present actions too – specifically with regard to the impact these actions had and have. The reasons for some observations we make may not be 100 per cent clear because other people's actions or sheer luck (or misfortune) can play a vital role in success or failure. Thus uncertainty can be connected to the future, the past and the present.

WHAT WILL HAPPEN?

The most obvious link with time is uncertainty regarding future developments. A lot of research accumulates around this issue. Many of the examples discussed in this book are related to issues of predicting the future. What will the weather be like tomorrow? What result will the next throw of a coin or dice yield? Research typically focuses on questions such as: Can we forecast what will happen in the future? What are possible future scenarios for our decision problem? What is the confidence of our predictions?

Uncertainty is a fundamental and inherent concept of the future. We do not know what will happen or how things will pan out, and yet our actions now influence the future fundamentally. Hugh Courtney (2001) conceptualised these thoughts in his work on 20/20 foresight. The idea behind 20/20 foresight is to make the best possible choices about future strategy and vision considering the uncertainty you and your organisation face. And in order to do so, you need to understand the uncertainty and particularly the level of knowledge you are lacking. This does not mean that we can always eliminate all uncertainty and make our decisions based on perfect predictions, but it does mean that we understand what we do not know and understand the future as best we can.

Hugh Courtney differentiates four levels of uncertainty which you can see in Figure 8.1. These are: (1) a clear enough future, (2) a set of futures, (3) a range of futures, and (4) ignorance. He identified these from different industrial sectors that move and change at different speeds and thus demonstrate different levels of predictability. Based on this level of predictability different levels of uncertainty for making decisions and forecasting the future arise.

Level 1 uncertainty describes a clear enough future. You may not have all information you need so there remains some small level of uncertainty (depicted as a grey shade around the black line), but you know well enough what is likely to happen. Think for example of your favourite restaurant: you may not know exactly what the waiter's mood is or which ingredients are

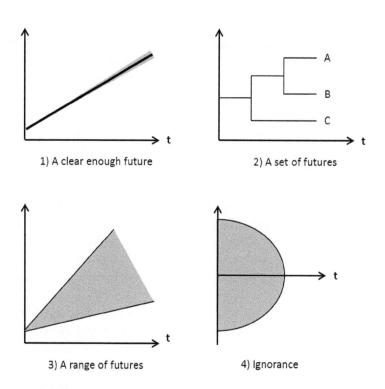

FIGURE 8.1 LEVELS OF UNCERTAINTY

available for the dish you order, but you know well enough that you will like what you get. For organisations, these situations occur in information-rich and mature markets. Think for example of the real-estate market in a well-established neighbourhood or the pricing decision of a new product for well-established brands. Consider Siemens, Coca-Cola or Volkswagen. They know their market segment relatively well and often have well-defined products to fit this market. They thus face low uncertainty when making these decisions.

Level 2 uncertainty describes a set of future outcomes. This set consists of a number of distinct possible outcomes for a problem or a decision. Think of throwing dice or flipping a coin. You have six and two distinct possible outcomes – a set of different futures. In an organisational context, this level of uncertainty is relatively rare: in practice there are rarely only a few distinct possible outcomes. One example is policy decisions – resulting for example from the choice of future governments. During the pre-election period, two or more contenders with different ideas for the future policy compete against each other, and each of these ideas for future policy has different implications for organisations – a set of possible futures.

The most likely or most often observed level of uncertainty is where you have an interval of future outcomes. You may be able to predict a maximum and a minimum value or scenario – like a best and worst case – and accept that any observation between the scenarios is possible. Imagine you are giving a party and you are planning the shopping you need to do for drinks and food and one major concern is the number of guests. You are uncertain about the exact number of guests you will have, but you know that some of your friends will definitely turn up. This is your minimum value. You also know how many people you have invited and can thus work out the maximum number of guests. Any number in between is possible, so you face level 3 uncertainty in your shopping decisions. Similarly, an organisation that is developing a new product or service and tries to predict the customer demand faces level 3 uncertainty. It may be able to define a minimum and maximum value – an optimistic and a pessimistic scenario – with reasonable confidence levels. But the possible range is large enough to cause some trouble for the strategic decision maker in the company.

Under ignorance – or level 4 uncertainty – no reasonable predictions can be made about the future. Things change so fast that tomorrow can already look completely different from today. Things may be so complicated and complex that you are incapable of even defining what the different factors are that contribute to a specific future. Many students face a situation like this when they come towards the end of their undergraduate studies and are close to graduation. When they do not have a potential employer lined up, there is often an abundance of possible career tracks to move into and each of them include their own range of possibilities. They could work in a consultancy, in different career paths in industry or stay at university for a postgraduate course. For many it is also not clear in which country or on which continent they will follow their career: a situation of ignorance about the future.

Uncertainty surrounds most of our choices regarding the future, but it can also be connected to the past and the present. Time is asymmetric: we may be able to see the past but we can not influence it. In contrast, we cannot see the future but we can influence it. Uncertainty can also be connected to the past and present. This is what we look at in the following sections.

WHAT DID HAPPEN?

Theoretically, we are not uncertain about the past – we have experienced it and this knowledge should be stored somewhere. So the information is available. Theoretically. In practice, this is not always the case. What did you do on 13 October 2014? To answer this question, many of us need to consult a calendar or other notes to remember. We are uncertain about the answer although technically, we should not be. We have experienced the past and thus have all the relevant knowledge and information. But sometimes we do not.

In Chapter 2, Perceiving uncertainty, we talked about a situation where you have been on holiday with a friend or spouse and try to describe your experiences to someone else after you return. The point we were making in Chapter 2 was that we perceive situations differently – the story you tell will differ (slightly) from the story your friend or spouse tells. This example is useful for the discussions we will have in this chapter. When we try to recall details about specific events in the past, we often find that we are unable to do so. Even when you have just come back from your holiday, you may already miss out some details of your experience, and the longer ago the said holiday was in the past, the fewer details you will remember about it.

This means that we can be uncertain about the past, and we often are. We try to document as much as possible. In holidays we take photos on all the main sights and places to remind us later of the great experiences we have had. But we cannot document everything – for practical and technical reasons. Thus we need to make choices of what to document and what not. It is often difficult to make this choice because we do not know which information we will need or want in the future. When Stewart Brand (1999) described his thoughts about building and stocking a library for future generations to document our lives now, he remarked: "*You never know* what will be treasured later" (emphasis in the original). Thus relevant and important information about the past may be lost, so we are uncertain about these events and experiences.

For organisations, these considerations can be relevant in multiple ways. One obvious example is legal responsibility as some information has to be recorded and submitted to the relevant authorities for review. Consider for example company taxes based on previous profits and cash flow. Issues of fraud and responsibility are often examples of uncertainty because some relevant information was not recorded or deliberately embezzled.

WHAT IS HAPPENING?

We can be uncertain about the future and about the past. We can even be uncertain about the present. Situations may be so complex that we can only really understand them when we see which factors are important in determining success or failure. Imagine you are trying to choose between different universities for your continued education. You may be worried about the quality of the education at the universities under consideration, the cost of attending the courses, living expenses in the city and your future employability once you have completed the course. These factors may be influenced by the quality of staff employed at the universities, political and strategic considerations, and the reputation of the university amongst companies and other organisations, your future lifestyle as a student and so on. There are a large number of factors that you will most likely be unable to know in detail and with precision. You are uncertain about the present.

Uncertainty about the present can often be reduced. We can try to collect as much information as possible to make an informed decision. To choose a good university for your continued education, you may look at their statistics – the percentage of students who found employment straight after graduating from the universities you are considering, or you may talk to a few graduates about their experiences. There is a lot you can do to reduce uncertainty but typically, some uncertainty remains. This is what researchers call residual uncertainty – the part that is left over after trying to collect further information.

Residual uncertainty remains because what you do not know may be unknowable. To know that 95 per cent of students are very happy studying at a certain university does not guarantee that you would be if you studied there. Similarly, to know that it takes the graduates from a university an average of 10 months to find a job does not guarantee that you would find one. Knowing that some of the students start their own businesses after graduating from the university you are considering does not mean that you would be able to create a successful start-up. You could only find these things out when you go and experience them yourself. Otherwise, this information is unknowable to you.

Another reason for the existence of residual uncertainty may be economic or time constraints. It usually takes a lot of both – time and money – to gather further information. You need to go to the universities homepage to find the statistics about their graduates. You need to talk to some graduates to get their first-hand experiences. And this might involve travel. All these activities cost time and money, and at some point you may just have to make a decision with the information you have.

Organisations also face uncertainty and can engage in various approaches to reduce this uncertainty, but often there remains some uncertainty that they simply have to deal with. They also face residual uncertainty that they might not be able to reduce at all – because the information they need is unknowable – or because they cannot (or do not want to) spend extra money and time on acquiring additional information. The first-mover advantage often keeps them from resolving uncertainty completely. It is often impossible to simply wait until uncertainty has resolved itself or avoid dealing with uncertainty all together. Thus uncertainty in the present is very important and deserves consideration and attention.

Everything Changes

One good way to analyse the link between uncertainty and time in organisations is looking at projects. Projects stand out because they are time constraint. They are formed with a purpose or goal in mind and disappear when this purpose or goal has been achieved. Some projects even have a predefined life span when they are formed. For example, Master's and Bachelor's projects at universities typically have a set length of five or six months. After this time, the project comes to a conclusion whether the student has reached the goal or not.

Organisations often do things in projects when they have a specific goal. This goal can be the development of a new piece of equipment or technology, or to implement new software that will change how information is recorded and communicated within an organisation. Thus a project is a temporary organisation that works on achieving this goal in a given time span.

Projects have a life cycle of their own. In the beginning, projects are initiated and created, the project partners are assembled and the project team created.

Then comes the planning phase where the goal is broken down into activities and responsibilities of the project partners. These activities are executed in the next and often longest project phase – the execution phase. Finally, the project is closed and achievements are compared to targets and goals.

Uncertainty can develop over these project phases. It can arise and be resolved. In theory, the development of uncertainty over the different project phases can be described in an uncertainty cone. The uncertainty cone says that at the beginning of a project the uncertainty is highest because the goal may be unknown or unclear; the roles of the stakeholders have to be defined and clarified and so on. Over the duration of a project, this uncertainty resolves as issues are identified and solved. The project goal (slowly) becomes clearer and the project partners get to know each other and build trust. Uncertainty is reduced. Figure 8.2 shows the uncertainty cone.

As usual, the reality looks a little different than the theory because reality depends on our perceptions. And the perception of uncertainty over time has not been tested explicitly. This is especially surprising because so many academic works depends on this overarching assumption – the assumption that uncertainty is highest in the beginning and reduces over time. Just wait. We decided to give this assumption a reality test and see how uncertainty perception actually develops over a project.

In 2014 I together with some fellow researchers undertook a project to look at how uncertainty evolves over the phases of projects. We chose one

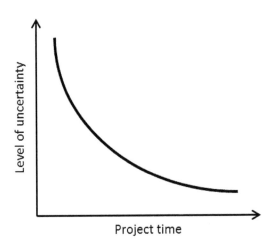

FIGURE 8.2 UNCERTAINTY CONE

particular type of project, a change project. Change projects are inherently uncertain. When an organisation decides to change part of its processes – by implementing new software or changing the overall company strategy or moving into a new property – it inevitably discovers unchartered territory. Things remain undefined and unknown. What exactly will the future strategy look like? What are the implications for employees? How will things be done in the future? Uncertainty is always part of defining a change, and part of the change project is to recognise and manage this uncertainty over time.

CHANGING THE LAYOUT AND CHANGING THE PROCESS

We investigated a change project where an organisation had decided to implement a new Enterprise Resource Planning (ERP) system. Let us call this organisation Company X. Essentially, an ERP system is a new piece of software that can integrate many existing applications of how to record and store organisational information such as material orders from suppliers, shipments to customers, payroll to employees and so on. Company X's main aim was to make information recording and sharing between their departments more efficient and transparent. The initial change would simply be to design and implement a new piece of software but the knock-on effects would be huge because the new piece of software would enable this company to do things differently in the future. This would be a big change for Company X.

This big change caused high levels of uncertainty for the company. What would be the requirements of the new ERP system? Company X had no background in software development, so a software developer had to be involved. The software developer had no idea what it was that Company X wanted or how their processes worked, and neither party knew how much the processes of Company X would change after the implementation of the ERP system. Should the system simply replicate the current systems? Could some changes already be anticipated and hence included in the new ERP system? Who should use it? How would the information flow between departments? Who would have access to what part of the database? These questions were difficult to answer and created much uncertainty for the project team and Company X.

We showed in Chapter 7 that organisations face various uncertainty types. Project uncertainty can arise from missing clear project goals or knowing exactly in advance what the project will deliver. Organisational uncertainty means that an organisation may not have all the capabilities it needs to fulfil a specific task or deliver a certain output. Relational uncertainty exists in every interorganisational relationship when two or more partners collaborate for a joint goal, and environmental uncertainty arises from the fact that economies move and technologies advance. Company X also faced these different uncertainty types in different levels of intensity.

Project uncertainty arose because Company X did not know the specifications of the final ERP solution. They neither knew what an ERP system could bring to the table, nor what their future needs would be after processes had changed. And Company X did not trust outside partners enough to involve them at this early stage. So they tried to define a list of technical and project requirements themselves – by calling a group of employees to the table to brainstorm these requirements. After a long process, they ended up with a list of almost 2000 requirements, yet many things remained unclear.

Organisational uncertainty arose for Company X because they had no background in software development and could thus not complete the task of implementing a new ERP system by themselves. They used the initial list of almost 2000 technical and project requirements to find a suitable software developer. The software developer would help and support Company X with implementing the new ERP system and complement the lacking organisational capabilities.

This partnering up with an external company inevitably created relational uncertainty. Company X found a suitable software developer but they had never worked together before. The software developer's performance would be measured against the initial list of requirements – this was what they had to deliver. The software developer was only involved in the change project after its start – when the project was planned and the timeline was set. Yet with their experience in ERP systems and software development, the software developer soon discovered that the list of requirements was not sufficient – it did not define the future ERP project in enough detail and lacked some functionality that would add value for Company X.

So the list of requirements was amended and one by one, new requirements were added and old ones taken off the list. However, the relationship between Company X and the software developer was set and meant to be managed by the original requirements list. After all, this was what the software developer was contracted to deliver. As this deliverable was amended one step at a time so the relationship had to be redefined and arrangements for the new deliverable agreed.

Long story short: the ERP project did deliver and a new ERP solution was implemented in Company X. The system fulfilled the amended requirements list. As a total change project, it can be seen as a success. The change was implemented and delivered success for Company X. However, the project was delayed from the original time plan. Deliverables started not being met as soon as the project was executed and these delays added up in the end.

Uncertainties added up as the project went along. And our analysis focused on this part of the change project: how uncertainty developed over the progress of the change project.

UNCERTAINTY AND PROJECT PHASES

The ERP implementation project followed the typical project phases. First, they initiated the project. Then they planned it and specified tasks and schedules. Third, they executed the project and established the ERP solution. Finally, the solution was implemented in Company X. All of this was supposed to happen in 11 months – from start to finish.

The uncertainty types descried above – project uncertainty, organisational uncertainty and relational uncertainty – fluctuated over the duration of the project. Figure 8.3 shows this fluctuation. Project uncertainty remained high over the whole duration of the project. Company X only realised the "true" level of their lack of knowledge about the project goals when they started to change the initial list of technical and project requirements. This revealed their lack of understanding of the true goal of the change project.

Company X lacked in-house capabilities to fulfil the project aim – they lacked software development skills. This meant that organisational uncertainty was high in the early stage of the change project. By bringing in an external partner, they aimed at reducing this uncertainty. In the last stages of the change project, organisational uncertainty increased again as the ultimate impact of

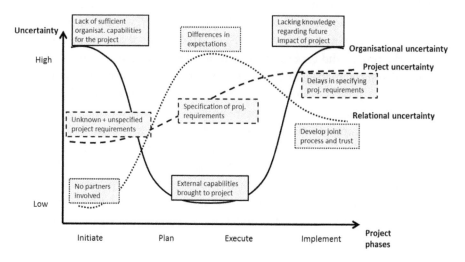

FIGURE 8.3 DEVELOPMENT OF UNCERTAINTY TYPES OVER TIME

the project became relevant and Company X realised its lack of understanding of the changes the ERP system would bring to the company. Would some people have to be let go? Would some departments be made redundant? This created an air of uncertainty.

Relational uncertainty started when the software developer was brought on board. The partners did not know each other prior to the project so relational uncertainty was high. After some time, they started to get to know each other and gain trust and subsequently the relational uncertainty was reduced.

One of the curious parts of this project is the lack of environmental uncertainty. In our research, we did not find any observations of environmental uncertainty. We can attribute this to the short time period that this project spans – 11 months. This is relatively short to record technological advancements. No major market developments were observed. But what we can assume is that environmental uncertainty had an impact on the decision to implement the ERP system in the first place. Strategic decision-making like that usually translates information from the company's context into the organisation. Thus, on the project level, environmental uncertainty has limited if no impact.

HOW SPECIAL IS COMPANY X?

This is one case. One company and one change project that we followed for this research. What does this look like for other companies? How generalisable are these findings? Research tells us that about 70 per cent of change projects fail. In one way or another, the project goals are never realised. The project we followed was deemed a success. The ERP system was defined and implemented. So this puts Company X in the top third of organisational change projects.

Yet the project did experience significant delays. This is a relatively typical feature of project management. If we were to believe the figures, it is more surprising if a project is delivered on time than if we experience delays. One might almost state that no one expects projects to deliver on time. So our ERP project from Company X fits right into the literature. And uncertainty – or the lack of recognising the true level and characterisation of the uncertainty in a change project – might be the key to explaining the statistics of large-scale delays.

We need more insights in this area. How does uncertainty perception develop in other types of projects? Say, for example, a product development project, a construction project or even a research project? Is there an overall trend for the development of the different uncertainty types or does this development depend on the specific project – like a project fingerprint in uncertainty form? These and many other questions remain to be answered.

CHAPTER 9

Uncertainty in Organisational Decision Making

In 2005, the Danish newspaper *Jyllands Posten* published editorial cartoons depicting the prophet Muhammad, a decision which would anger many Muslims around the globe. This caused almost immediate political outrage as eleven ambassadors of Muslim countries complained to the Danish prime minister about what they perceived to be an insult on their religion and culture. Some local groups even filed criminal complaints for investigation. The cartoons were reprinted in Norwegian, French, German, Icelandic, Italian, Belgian and Swiss newspapers amongst others and even found their way to Jordan and New Zealand media. This started a heated debate about political and religious conflicts and freedom of speech.

In the meantime, consumers in countries such as Saudi Arabia boycotted Danish products and even removed them from their supermarket shelves. The boycott soon escalated across the Middle East. The Denmark-based dairy firm Arla was particularly badly hit by these boycotts and lost up to €1.3 million a day in sales. Despite the fact that Arla had little to do with the origins of the crisis and almost no control over its development and proportions, they were badly hit in the aftermath.

Decision making in all different kinds of organisations and at different managerial levels determined the further progression and proportions of the crisis. In their 2009 article, researchers from the University of Otago analysed the events and identified the key decision points that could have led to a de-escalation of the crisis for Arla and other affected companies. The decisions that were made by different people involved in this widely spread and complex network of actors and organisations increased the severity step-by-step, as shown in Figure 9.1. At every decision point, the involved actors would (hopefully) carefully consider all the options and available information before commencing on the course the crisis eventually took. Yet given the uniqueness and unprecedented nature of this situation, the uncertainty is unimaginably high, creating difficulties in determining which option is the right way ahead.

Making Regular Decisions

Not all situations that organisations face are as unique as the one described above. One of my earlier research studies focused on the uncertainty that organisations face when they bid competitively to become a provider of engineering services. We talked in some of the earlier chapters (Chapter 7 for example) about servitized manufacturers – manufacturing companies that increasingly use engineering services such as maintenance for their products to compete on the market, similar to when a car manufacturer also provides some maintenance support.

Many of these engineering service contracts are given after a process of competitive bidding – where different companies who (think they) have the

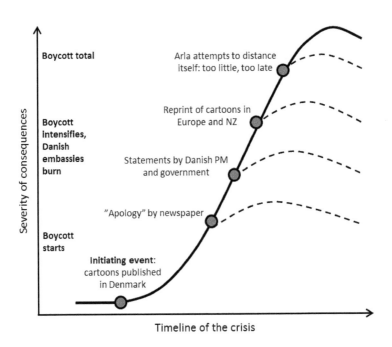

FIGURE 9.1 TIMELINE OF THE MUHAMMAD CARTOON CRISIS[1]

1   This is a simplified version of events as described by Knight, J.G., Mitchell, B.S. and Gao, H., 2009. Riding out the Muhammad Cartoons Crisis : Contrasting Strategies and Outcomes. *Long Range Planning*, 42(1), pp. 6–22.

capabilities to provide the requested service bid to become the contracted service provider. They compete not only on the contract price, for example the annual fee for the service, but also on other factors such as frequency of inspections, geographical network of service engineers, technical know-how or innovativeness of the procedures. In short, the decisions that the potential providers have to take consist of various factors which are constrained by the company's level of existing capabilities, which are intertwined in complex ways and in turn create uncertainty regarding bidding success and optimal bidding strategy.

My study aimed at identifying how this uncertainty impacts the decision-making process of the potential providers for these service contracts. Following interviews with responsible decision makers in different companies, I identified different decision-making patterns, and some of the observations I made surprised me immensely and would shape the way I would design future research studies.

TALKING UNCERTAINTY

I contacted and sampled the companies and interviewees with the purpose of talking about uncertainty in their decision-making processes. Thus the participants were happy to talk about their practices for identifying uncertainty, managing risk and collecting information. Each of the interviews started with the question regarding the participants' understandings and definitions of the terms uncertainty and risk – to form a basis for our discussions. While I expected the need to be flexible in my own definition of the terms – which invariably resulted from reading the academic literature in the field and engaging in many academic discussions with colleagues – I did not expect the breadth of business practice.

In particular, I still remember one interviewee who would not let himself be pinned down to a particular definition of the terms or to articulating a difference between uncertainty and risk. Instead, he always followed my lead in his answers – when I phrased the question containing the term uncertainty, he would exclusively use uncertainty in his answer and vice versa with risk. I was startled by this observation, and as you can imagine it posed significant difficulties in discussing the issue and the interviewee's organisational decision-making processes under uncertainty.

While this was clearly a more extreme case, most of the participants in this study found it difficult to identify a difference in the terms and clarify the practical implications this has for their businesses, processes and decision making. Often we would discuss specific examples of risk events such as the risk of a red light during a car journey or the loss of a team member whose knowledge is central to the fulfilment of the service. This clarifies the implicit assumption that risk contains some sort of an impact and the extent of this impact determines a suitable approach to managing it.

It contrast, uncertainty often had a much more subjective connotation which can be identified and managed through the experience and knowledge of the responsible manager and their team. Thus it seems that organisations – at least the sample that I interviewed – have a very subjective approach to dealing with uncertainty which relies heavily on the experience and ability of their senior managers.

WHAT DO WE ALREADY KNOW?

In line with this understanding, I found that much of the existing knowledge about uncertainty consisted of the subjective experience of managers, engineers and decision makers in the organisation. Knowing the customer, their aims with the service contract – including things such as the terminology they use to express their needs and requirements, the key decision makers and their preferences in evaluating offers as well as their strategy – can reduce uncertainty and thus help in making the right decision.

During the bidding process, any informal communications between a potential provider and their customer are typically forbidden – or if they do happen are public to all involved parties (i.e. potential competitors have a right to participate and follow the exchange). Thus not much information is exchanged once the bidding process starts, which means that the potential providers have to rely on the information they already have. This information can come from the bid advertisement (i.e. the official bidding documentation that lists the service requirements and often also the evaluation criteria). Most valuable, though, is the information that comes from the experience and market knowledge of managers, engineers and decision makers within the potential provider's organisation.

The managers experience comes from the history of the organisation and its employees on the market and the industrial sector. Having engaged in competitive bidding processes before, they know who the main competitors are, the context of the bidding process and the customer's evaluation, and they may even know the customer's prior experience in receiving a service and working with different providers. Having participated in other bidding processes – and most importantly having learned from these experiences – means that bidding decision makers have an idea with regard to which competitor might underbid them, what their competitors main capabilities are and thus what level of service quality they are likely to offer.

Based on this experience, the interviewees also stated that they try to evaluate the future. This concerns possible future needs of the customer that they can include in their bid to support the customer's operations and to improve their chances of winning the process. This also concerns their competitors' future strategies and thus determines their own competitive position on the market. Thus the organisation's experience and particularly the managers' subjective knowledge has an important part to play in competitive bidding decisions.

Other sources of information – evaluations of previous bidding projects and existing service contracts – may be stored in databases. My study participants did mention this information source but it was used much less frequently than the subjective approaches described above. This finding seems logical as services are relatively unique encounters – especially in a business-to-business context. Different service contracts differ from each other because they depend on the specific customer (and conversely on the specific provider), their utilisation rates of the serviced equipment, the level of interaction between provider and customer, their degree of prior engagement and frequency and depth of communication. Thus information stored in databases can give only limited insights into the specific bidding process at hand and reduce the uncertainty in the decision-making process.

DECISION-MAKING PROCESSES

I found that the decision-making process in competitive bidding relies heavily on the subjective evaluations by decision makers and managers. Their subjective judgement is a core source of information as well as a core managerial tool for evaluating the uncertainty in the decision-making process. In addition, some more objective or formal managerial tools can be used, such as modelling techniques using tools like Monte Carlo analysis or sensitivity analysis to evaluate how susceptible the evaluations are to variations in the input values. These tools can support the subjective assessments by offering more objective decision support; however, subjective approaches seem to dominate in practice.

This has advantages and disadvantages. Relying on experience and knowledge means that costly computations and access to large databases can be circumvented. Also, the experience and knowledge can be internalised using existing approaches to organisational learning. Specifically in many situations where objective data is missing, decisions can still be made with a reasonable level of confidence as managers are used to utilising their experience and relying on their subjective assessment of a situation.

On the other hand, organisational decision-making processes are also susceptive to the decision-making biases listed in Chapter 5 which make it likely that decisions are based on misperceptions, overconfidence and misjudgements. Managers are human and are thus prone to making the same errors as other people in situations of uncertainty. They are likely to rely overly on recent past experiences, orient themselves towards an anchor value, search for information that confirms their assumptions and ignore information that contradicts these assumptions. And what is worse, these effects are likely to affect decision makers simultaneously to varying degrees. The relative importance of the impact of these decision-making biases may determine the decision outcome and ultimately the business success.

Thus it is important to drive the research in this area further and enhance our understanding of organisational decision making under uncertainty. The activation mechanisms – stating that we only use "activated" information in our decision-making process – may be a suitable theory to explain the observations we make in practice. However, the research in this area needs much further development and the insights from field such as psychology seem relevant and insightful to furthering our understanding in this field.

Irregular Circumstances

Apart from the regular business challenges many organisations face, we also see an increasing number of irregular challenges where crises and turbulences make business as usual untenable. Events such as the Arab Spring, the Hong Kong protests in 2014, the 2011 Fukushima crisis or the Muhammad cartoon crisis in 2005 usually start locally but soon develop a global impact and can cause severe breakdowns to business processes and operations. Supplies are disrupted, financing is not available, staff don't show up to work or their safety is not guaranteed. Close-knit and widely branched business networks mean that these disruptions ripple through the system and cause unpredictable impacts around the globe.

Events like these often take on a life of their own and can threaten the viability of organisations. While the fundamental starting points of these crises can differ hugely with natural catastrophes such as the 2011 tsunami in Japan or human-induced events such as the 2014 Hong Kong protests, their characteristics are often the same. A sequence of events following the starting point increase the volume and complexity with increasing speed which means that events soon spiral out of control and create huge difficulties for managers and organisations.

Challenging circumstances create situations of high uncertainty. These crises often create challenges for organisations that have little or no control over events. Causes and effects are difficult to determine and even more importantly, means of resolving the difficulties are not clear or easy to establish. Who is responsible (or should be held responsible) when contractual arrangements fail in these circumstances? How can their impact be limited? Corporate mismanagement can have devastating impacts and intensify the problems.

Some researchers have even recommended that in some situations, managers need to simply "ride out the storm" and try not to actively manipulate the situation because any actions may make things worse. However, this is what many managers are bad at. They prefer to predict the future, creating comprehensible scenarios of the decisions they can take and the impact these have. They want to know what to expect. During crises, however, this is often not possible as managers find themselves in unprecedented situations that change constantly and have the potential to escalate rapidly. They create small areas of certainty that can be handled. Thus many organisational decision makers often respond to crises and situations of high uncertainty in the opposite to what has been predicted to work and lead to greater effectiveness, and their experiencing of uncertainty is at the heart of this issue. The ingrained thinking of managers and organisations needs to be unfrozen to allow for new ways of thinking and deciding under uncertainty. Uncertainty is prevalent and dealing with this uncertainty in their decision making is a great challenge for organisations.

One example of such an irregular event was the 2008–2009 global financial crisis. Following the burst of the US housing bubble, the value of securities reduced drastically and many large financial institutions were on the brink of collapse. These collapses were often only prevented through bailouts by national governments to prevent further damage to the economy and stability. In 2008, the UK Treasury injected £37 billion into banks such as the Royal Bank of Scotland and Lloyds TSB while Germany signed a €450 billion deal to bail out its banks. Stock markets were shaken, investments stagnated, unemployment increased, the gross domestic product (of GDP) of many Western economies slowed down and world trade declined. Experts estimate that this crisis has been the worst since the great depression in the 1930s.

The crisis created high levels of uncertainty for many economies and many organisations. It showed the huge amplitude that macroeconomic fluctuations can obtain. In Europe alone most economies struggled with the impact the crisis had on their GDPs (see Figure 9.2 for the budget deficit and public debt to GDP for selected EU countries in 2009). One economy after the other faltered as Greece, Ireland, Portugal, Spain and Cyprus had to request bailout programmes from the International Monetary Fund (IMF).

Many organisations faced the uncertainty the crisis created for them and managed to escape the very real possibility of failure and bankruptcy. Working with a small research team, we designed a study to look at how organisations that were impacted by the events reacted to the uncertainty it created. We interviewed managers of different organisations – large and small, private businesses and non-for-profit organisations – about their experience with the

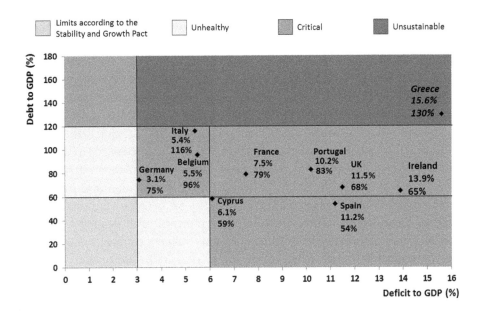

FIGURE 9.2 BUDGET DEFICIT AND PUBLIC DEBT OF SELECTED EUROPEAN COUNTRIES IN 2009[2]

2   Source: Eurostat, adapted from: https://upload.wikimedia.org/wikipedia/commons/1/1a/ Budget_Deficit_and_Public_Debt_to_GDP_in_2009_%28for_selected_EU_Members%29. png

crisis and the decisions they made to escape the possible devastating impact on their organisations. And we received some really interesting insights into their view of events.

WHAT UNCERTAINTY TYPES DID THEY PERCEIVE?

As we expected, the study participants highlighted the high levels of uncertainty in the wake of the financial crisis. In particular, environmental uncertainty was high on the agenda as markets were changing rapidly with stock prices fluctuating vastly and on a daily basis. Prices for commodities such as oil plummeted, causing high variations in demand as well as supply. This made predictions and subsequent management very difficult because a stable basis for the decisions was missing.

What surprised us was the description of politics and the impact that changes in regulations and laws had on organisations. Regulatory uncertainty arising from possible changes in the rules and regulations was a major source of uncertainty quoted by the interviewees. The financial crisis motivated governments around the world to change the regulations of their banking systems in order to prevent a similar crisis from happening again in the (near) future. These regulations also impacted organisations in other industrial sectors such as companies operating in transport and logistics, technology, and public administration and defence. Thus the nature of the regulations, the timing of their implementation and the impact on their business processes was a source of uncertainty for organisations following the global financial crisis.

DECISION-MAKING PROCESSES IN A CRISIS

Unsurprisingly, organisational decision-making processes varied immensely. These were mainly influenced by the type of environment the organisation operated in: whether rapid changes and developments require rapid responses, whether reliability of decisions is the main priority requiring high confidence levels based on trustworthy information, or whether there simply is not enough information available and experience remains the core decision-making variable. The industrial setting and requirements determine much about the organisational decision-making processes and degree to which uncertainty can and has to be considered. Thus different organisations use different processes to make their decisions.

Our study found that the majority of respondents tried to use some form of decision support in the form of models or data-driven forecasts. This is surprising when we compare these results to the study I described above where organisations involved in bidding decisions (a relatively regular or at least reoccurring process in many organisations) rely on the judgement and experience of their decision makers. In other words, in regular processes, uncertainty is considered in the organisational decision-making process through subjective sense-making of the decision maker while in irregular circumstances, model-based approaches are prevalent. This is a surprising finding in irregular situations; less data is available because the events and situations they created are unique.

Yet this finding is explainable with some of the insights that psychology research gives us and that we discussed in Part I of this book. Situations of high levels of uncertainty create an emotional response in us and often this response is related to negative feelings such as fear. In managers this fear can create the need to rely on some form of decision support in order to benchmark the evaluations and expectations for the future. Whether the models give a sufficiently accurate prediction was not part of our study, but what they do seem to offer is some form of security for the decision maker because they give a ballpark idea and an overall anchor for the decision-making process.

We have to acknowledge that the type of decisions we looked at in the two studies (the competitive bidding study and the global financial crisis study) differ because the available information, level of uncertainty, organisational levels and type of decision makers are different. The described findings give some interesting insights that spark further questions for future studies, but the findings align with phenomena other researchers describe in irregular circumstances.

In highly uncertain situations, we often create small islands of certainty which can be handled in managerial decision making. We can set small goals and make plans to reach them. These smaller decision-making problems can then be solved by following rules of thumb, using existing and proven processes and relying on existing patterns, reducing the fear and making the situation more controllable and predictable. We can then use traditional methods to support the decision making as models can handle the small islands of certainty. The problem of irregular circumstances is simplified by ignoring some of the complexities and uncertainties. This enables us to still reach organisational goals without encountering difficulties along the way – at least in theory.

In practice, this approach is often not good enough. Harold L. Wilensky described this as "conditions that foster the failure in foresight". This quote comes from his publication in 1967, but it is still relevant – maybe now even more so. Ignoring some of the complexities in challenging circumstances can create huge problems for organisations. Uncertainty is a central part in that process as it enables these activities, but we have to be comfortable with the notion that we often simply do not know all the information needed to make the optimal decision.

COMMUNICATING DURING CHALLENGING CIRCUMSTANCES

Effective communication is a crucial element in almost all successful crisis management efforts. Poor communication can make a bad situation even worse. When decision makers use models to support their decision-making processes in irregular circumstances or in crises, the output needs to be communicated to them in such a way that they can understand the underlying assumptions, and comprehend the suggestions the model gives and uncertainties it includes. In addition, managers need to communicate in these circumstances and make sense to the relevant people.

This raises an important question: Who are the relevant people? Who needs to be communicated with and what information do they need? Internal communications within organisations are needed to keep operations running and support the relevant processes. Our study participants highlighted the issue of changes in staff during irregular circumstances – either through lay-offs to save costs or through restructuring and relocations of existing staff. Making sure that a new employee receives the information they need and understands the messages they require was one of the main communication challenges of managers.

External communications are often also crucial during challenging times. The public may need to be kept updated on events; gatekeepers to suppliers, customers, government or local authorities may require information and can in turn be an important source of information for organisations. Communication is one of the core tools to overcome crises and the uncertainty they entail. Identifying when, what and with whom to communicate requires managers to make sense in situations of high uncertainty. Yet little is known in managerial theory about this issue which means we researchers have a lot of catching up to do to satisfy the needs of current and future managerial practice.

Often, crises have a global character and concern people of different cultures, languages, religion, political attitudes and ethnical groups. This requires a strong sense of cultural sensitivity. One example is the 2005

Muhammad cartoon crisis that spread from a local newspaper in Denmark to a crisis of truly global proportions that involved organisations in Norway, Germany, New Zealand and the Middle East. Solving this crisis involved treating in unchartered territory for all involved parties, making sense of the situation, acting in a culturally sensitive way and most of all dealing with the uncertainty the situation created.

IN HINDSIGHT

We finished the interviews of our global financial crisis study with a question regarding the lessons learnt – What would managers do differently if they could relive the events following the crisis? Most of the answers we received were related to the organisational capabilities – having the right people available at the right time, more involvement between employees and with management to share experiences and knowledge. As we know more and more about our individual limitations in dealing with uncertainty and making the right decisions when we simply do not have enough information about the possible outcomes, sharing knowledge and engaging others in the decision-making process seems to become more and more important. Gathering different experiences and viewpoints on an issue can perhaps help overcome some of the limitations we face as individual decision makers.

Almost half of our interviewees acknowledged that they misinterpreted the uncertainty that came with the crisis. They were either too confident in their own abilities and thus took on projects that were too ambitious, defined activities that were too big and complex and were too optimistic in their own assessments. In many cases, this led to voidable project failures. On the other hand, some managers felt they overestimated uncertainty and were too doubtful of their own abilities. They took too long to make decisions or they did not trust in their own knowledge. While hindsight is always more comfortable than foresight, these findings clearly suggest that we still have a long way to go in understanding the role of uncertainty in managerial decision making: we need to improve our theoretical understanding of the impact of uncertainty on managerial decision making and come to terms with its importance in organisations.

CHAPTER 10

Taking Action in Organisations

Imagine you are a new entrant at a renowned investment bank. You have just finished your degree and are eager to apply what you have learned to reality, to prove yourself out there in the real world. You start your job and on your first day, you notice something is different. Instead of giving you clear instructions on what is expected from you – follow guidelines and do what you are told by your superiors – your new employer is giving you a lot of freedom. Where you thought you would simply execute decisions, you now have to make the decisions on which way to go in the first place. Instead of working with companies and industry sectors that are your speciality, you have to deal with cases of environments and problems that are new and completely unknown to you. You thought you would learn from the big names in your field, the "star players" of your bank, and instead you are working with different people on each project, sometimes with no senior colleagues involved at all.

This way of working is very confusing and stressful, and it is not what you are used to. Your university education led you to believe that you would always receive clear instruction on what to deliver and when to deliver it. You could reach your goals simply by working hard, being dedicated to your work and becoming the specialist in your field. You had your whole career planned out for yourself: a few years where you immerse yourself in your work and get established. You would have to put in 80–120 hours per week but it would be worth it: with this you would build the foundation of your whole career. You would find your passion and work in this area as hard as you can. Then, at some point, you would be the new "star player" in this field. A person to look up to. Your vision was clear – low uncertainty.

Yet here you are and nothing works according to your plan. Your bank was in fact amplifying uncertainty for you. You cannot build expertise in any one single area, let alone apply your experience to new projects. You have to think on your feet all the time, and most of your colleagues are in the same boat as you. You have to think of new strategies together and when these strategies succeed, it reflects positively on all of you. Not one single star player, but an organisation of many successful thinkers.

It takes some time, but after a few projects you are getting used to this way of working. Amplified uncertainty means also that no one expects you to have the right answers at all times. So asking colleagues is not a sign of weakness. Not knowing is not interpreted as incompetence. And once you get used to this way of working, you can see the excitement of the job – of working on completely new projects all the time, of working with a new group of people for every project and learning new ways of working together with every new group of people.

We Need to Know More!

As early as 1976, Barry A. Turner stated in one of his scholarly articles that "uncertainty creates problems for actions". Yet the insights we have produced in the scientific community over the last 40 years still leave amazing gaps to be filled. In Chapter 6, we talked about the possible actions we can take when we face uncertainty. In summary, these are (1) to reduce uncertainty by collecting further information and increasing our knowledge, (2) ignore uncertainty and act as if it did not exist, and (3) embrace uncertainty and use it creatively and innovatively.

In principle, organisations have the same choice for acting under uncertainty. They can aim to reduce uncertainty and they have multiple possibilities for doing so. They can collect new information and monitor their business environment for signals and new developments. They can also improve their internal information-processing capabilities – in essence make the communication between the departments more effective and efficient so that the available information reaches the persons who need it as fast as possible. Reducing uncertainty also means making sense of the new information, and in organisations this can be a more complicated task than for individuals.

Organisations can also ignore uncertainty, though the stakes of this action may be quite high. For example, if competitors do not ignore the environmental uncertainty and signals they receive from the market, they might be able to predict future markets and have the first-mover advantage. In the long run, this can even mean that an organisation that ignores uncertainty disappears from the landscape because they are not able to keep their customers and their market share. For this reason, organisations also have the possibility to insure against uncertainty and thus reduce their need to consider it in their decision making and action taking. We will look at some possibilities of how organisations can insure against uncertainty in this chapter.

The third option is to embrace uncertainty and pave the way to new markets and new opportunities. Many companies that are widely regarded as highly innovative have chosen this strategy. Think of Apple, for example, and their vision to make computers even more integrated into our daily lives. Despite harsh criticism from the community at the time, they launched the iPad and were thus the first company to open the tablet market.

We also learned in Chapter 6 that most research theory focuses on option number 1 – to reduce uncertainty. This is very much the same situation when we focus on organisations instead of individuals. According to the key researchers in the field – Jay Galbraith, Richard Daft and Robert Lengel – organisations respond to uncertainty by acquiring information and analysing data. The main purpose of managers is to understand the uncertainty and know which information they will need to look for. Organisational tools such as periodic reports, rules and procedures and regular meetings are aimed at improving communication within the organisation and thus help to reduce uncertainty.

In practice, this is not always the case. Some organisations know how to embrace and even increase the level of uncertainty they face by moving into uncharted territory, and this is yet another area where research has not caught up with practice – and reality – yet. In practice, it may be as important to know when you have to reduce uncertainty as it is to identify when to embrace or ignore it. Under uncertainty there is not always one best answer, and understanding when to go down a certain path and when to wait and see can bring an important advantage to organisations.

One of the ground-breaking works in this area was presented by Alexandra Michel and Stanton Wortham (2009) who collected rich insights from two different banks: one that followed the approach traditionally suggested by researchers, namely to reduce uncertainty wherever possible, and the other a bank that deliberately counteracts this approach and embraces uncertainty. Michel followed these two banks over a period of two years and collected what can only be described as an impressive amount of detailed and in-depth insight into their approaches to managing uncertainty. Their material spans observations of about 5–7 days of work with 80–120 hours per week, more than 130 semi-structured interviews and 120 unstructured interviews. Based on this vast and rich data, the two researchers present some really interesting findings of the role of uncertainty in organisations.

What they found was that two fundamentally different approaches to organisational uncertainty management – uncertainty reduction and uncertainty amplification – create fundamentally different environments for employees to interact, project work, client interaction and employee motivation and identification. Uncertainty reduction creates a clear environment for the individual. You are given clear expectations and indicators of what it means to reach these implications and to measure your performance against them. You know your role in your team and within the whole organisation. You know when and how you are expected to interact with clients and which clients you work with. You know your career path. These are all signs of an organisational approach to uncertainty reduction. Reducing uncertainty for the individual employee is a core task and enables you to do your job most effectively and efficiently.

In contrast, an organisation can intentionally amplify uncertainty. It can create situations where individual employees lack the clarity and knowledge about their expected actions. It can intentionally hold back on clear goals and performance measures, on lists of clients you are expected to work with. It can withhold clear job titles that detail what your role is in the organisation, in your team and in relation to projects. An organisation can intentionally throw their employees into new projects with unknown clients, in industrial contexts they have no or limited prior experience in and involve them in processes they have not seen before. You would miss clear details and expectations of your contribution as an employee, but you would gain the freedom to act and learn on your job as you see fit. You would be forced to face uncertainty and find and define your actions in the light of it. You would be given incentives to work with your colleagues to jointly interpret the situation and any new information that comes your way. You would initially feel very uncomfortable, but with time you may see the benefits of working with and benefitting from uncertainty.

Alexandra Michel and Stanton Wortham described two fundamentally different organisational approaches to handling uncertainty. Their assessment of these two organisations makes for a really interesting read because it challenges some of the fundamental assumptions we are given by many managerial theories and our university education. Their work focuses on the environments that organisations create for their employees with the approach they choose for handling uncertainty. In the following sections, we will look in more detail at how organisations can act based on the different types of uncertainty they can face.

I Know Where I Am

In much of my research I work with providers and customers of engineering services. These are companies that offer or receive support for their equipment and technology such as magnetic resonance imaging (MRI) scanners, water pumps, engines or even full production plants. The thought behind this arrangement is that the manufacturer of these pieces of equipment, have a lot of know-how about their equipment and are thus uniquely qualified to provide operational support. This includes regular inspections as well as finding faults and giving emergency support when needed.

Think for example of a company like Siemens Healthcare. They manufacture equipment for hospitals such as MRI scanners or computed tomography (CT) scanners but also smaller equipment for blood tests and so on. Imagine you work in a hospital and find that one of the scanners you work with does not function appropriately. The pictures you receive are blurry. What would you do? The hospital cannot afford to have a non-functional scanner for a long time so a solution needs to be found soon if not immediately. This is where having a service contract with the manufacturer of the scanner can come in handy. You simply call them and register the failure with the service provider, a company such as Siemens – and do not worry about it any more.

The service provider sends one of their service engineers to you in the hospital to look at the problem. A company like Siemens will have a distributed network of service engineers across the country or region. They would not dispatch someone from their head office – unless your hospital is actually close to their head office – but would send someone closer to you. That way, they can respond quickly and solve your problem immediately. Their service engineers are the core part of their service business.

ORGANISATIONAL UNCERTAINTY

This distributed network of engineers causes some organisational uncertainty: communication needs to be organised differently than if everyone works in the same office building and can catch each other up on the water cooler or while getting a cup of coffee. A lot of service engineers work from home and see their customers more often than their colleagues. Technology such as mobile phones, email and other communication channels help support this situation but often do not offer a complete substitute for face-to-face talks. One organisational challenge for providers of engineering services is to increase their capabilities for processing information between service engineers and make sure that information reaches the person who needs it.

A further organisational challenge arises from the pace of technological advances. Technical hospital equipment such as MRI scanners has an operational life of approximately 8 or 10 years. This means that some hospitals have old equipment while others have the latest technology installed. This creates challenges for the service engineers as they need to be able to handle, inspect and repair both old and new equipment, and need to be constantly aware of the latest technological developments. To reduce this organisational uncertainty, service providers such as Siemens give regular training sessions for their engineers to improve their technical skills and train them on the latest equipment.

RELATIONAL UNCERTAINTY

Service engineers are core to the business of providers of engineering services. They are the ones going to the hospitals and solving their problems. They are thus at the forefront of building and maintaining the relationship with the customer. They are core action-takers to resolve relational uncertainty. The relationship between service provider and the hospital stands or falls with them.

Many service engineers handle this responsibility by building close personal relationships with engineers, doctors and nurses at the hospitals whose equipment they service. Sometimes, these relationships may turn into friendships and in rare cases these friendships can span multiple decades. They often talk directly with each other. When a problem occurs, the member of staff at the hospital calls their dedicated engineer directly to come as quickly as possible and solve the problem.

This means that joint routines have to be established. During my work with different provider organisations of engineering services, one engineer – let us call him Tim – once told me his story of how he learned to work with a particularly difficult customer. He explained that this person, Paul, could be very disruptive to his work. Paul would often "pop in" on him servicing a piece of equipment, ask difficult questions and check exactly what Tim was doing. At some point – and by that time he would dread his visits to this company – Tim found out that Paul and his colleagues would go for a joint breakfast together at 10 a.m., visiting one of the mobile breakfast stalls around the corner. Going with them, Tim found that if he bought Paul a breakfast, Paul would leave him alone for the rest of the day. Tim explained to me: "For €5, I would gain peace for the rest of the day."

So establishing the customer's routine is another important action to resolving relational uncertainty. This can include personal routines, as the example with Paul showed, but it can also include organisational routines. To do a regular inspection on a MRI scanner, the service engineer would have to work around the patient schedule for treatments or appointments. Similarly, if an engine or even a whole production plant have to be serviced, the service engineers have to work around the usual production schedule as parts or the whole equipment have to be on a standstill.

These examples were all findings from cases where provider and customer operate in the same context. They were registered in the same country and were often even geographically located in the same region. This means that the legal framework applied to them, the same policy decisions, tax and payment schemes as well as unwritten values of doing business. Both organisations – customer and provider – are part of the same business culture and tradition. What happens to uncertainty when this constraint is lifted? When provider and customer are not only different organisations with different goals but also with different cultures and contexts?

I Don't Even Know Where To Go

Imagine a similar scenario to the one above: there is a manufacturer of equipment and they service this equipment for their customer. However, this time, both companies are situated in different countries and even on different continents. Imagine for the purpose of this example that the provider is originally positioned in northern Europe and the customer is stationed in Egypt. Figure 10.1 shows these two geographical positions of the provider and their customer on the world map.

There is a physical distance between the two organisations. There is also a cultural distance between them. In the 1990s, Samuel P. Huntington wrote about cultural zones or civilisations in our world. Each of these zones defines different sets of values that were mainly derived from religion and joint history. One example is Western culture where countries in Europe but also the USA, Canada and Australia have joint history and similar customs based on Christian values. In contrast, countries in North Africa such as Egypt belong to the Islamic culture, based on Muslim religion. Other zones are marked accordingly in Figure 10.1.

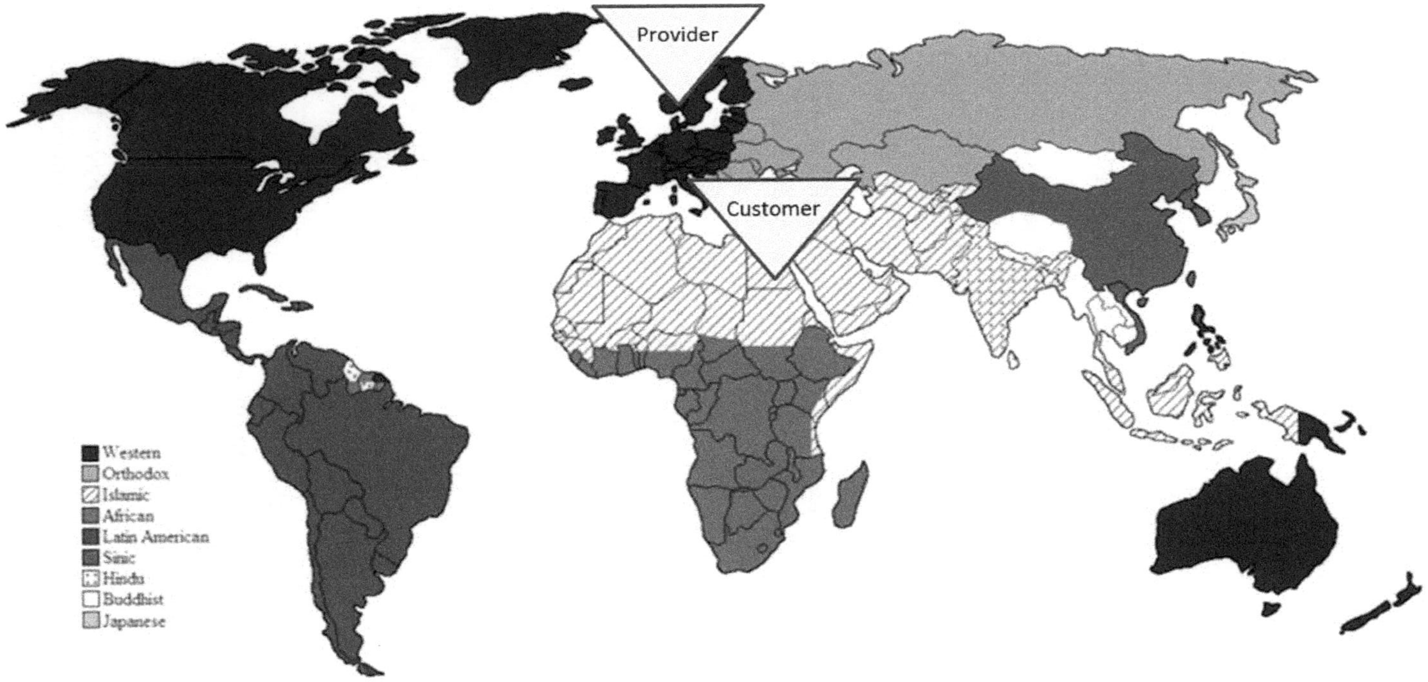

FIGURE 10.1 CROSS-CULTURAL BUSINESS VENTURES

While this is not supposed to be a lesson in history or religion, the works of Huntington show the fundamental cultural differences that underlie how things are done in different countries. To come back to our business example, our service provider wanted to provide services crossing these cultural zones. This meant not only that they faced obstacles in terms of language, legal systems, political systems and financial systems; they also had to get to know how the customer and organisations in general worked in Egypt. This was important for contract negotiations and implementation, installing the equipment, getting the relevant authorities to sign-off on the technology and building interpersonal relationships between service engineers and the customer staff. Uncertainty was an inherent part of this process.

ORGANISATIONAL UNCERTAINTY

We saw in the example above that a geographically close position to the customer is essential for services. This allows the service provider to respond quickly to call-outs. Thus the provider – positioned in northern Europe – built a local organisation in Egypt. This local representation would be situated close to the customer and could thus react to questions and problems. A daughter company with its own back office, service engineers and middle management. The staff was partly local – Egyptians with a background in engineering and services – and partly expats, experts from their head office with knowledge of the northern European mother company and organisational processes. This would bring the local organisation up to speed and help to run things smoothly. It would help the communication between the provider organisations and with the customer.

In the meantime, the provider faced the same organisational challenges as described above. Employee training and education were on the agenda and had to be managed remotely and through the local organisation. This education did not only concern technological advances but also management skills, and improving IT literacy and language skills. Corporate knowledge was English, and the language skills of everyone – including service engineers and other operational staff – had to be good enough to communicate both with the customer and with the head office in northern Europe.

RELATIONAL UNCERTAINTY

Apart from the difficulties connected to language and business culture, the local organisation also helped overcome relational uncertainty. Because of the

TABLE 10.1   COMPARISON OF NATIONAL CULTURES OF EGYPT AND SELECTED NORTHERN EUROPEAN COUNTRIES[1]

	Description	Egypt	Denmark	Norway	Iceland
Power distance	the degree to which the less powerful members of a society accept and expect that power is distributed unequally. People in societies with high values accept a hierarchical order. In societies with low values, people strive to equalise the distribution of power and demand justification for inequalities of power.	70	18	31	30
Individualism	the degree to which society is tightly or loosely knit. In societies with high values –called individualism – individuals are expected to take care of only themselves and their immediate families. In societies with low values – collectivism – individuals can expect their relatives or members of a particular in-group to look after them in exchange for unquestioning loyalty.	25	74	69	60
Career orientation (masculinity)	the degree to which a individuals in a society are competitive or consensus-oriented. Societies with high values (masculinity) prefer achievement, heroism, assertiveness and material rewards for success. Societies with low values (femininity) prefer cooperation, modesty, caring for the weak and quality of life.	45	16	8	10
Uncertainty avoidance	the degree to which the members of a society feel uncomfortable with uncertainty and ambiguity. Societies with high values maintain rigid codes of belief and are intolerant of unorthodox behaviour and ideas. Societies with low values maintain a more relaxed attitude in which practice counts more than principles.	80	23	50	50
Long-term orientation	the degree to which a society maintains links with its own past while dealing with the challenges of the present and the future. Societies with low values prefer to maintain time-honoured traditions and norms while viewing societal change with suspicion. Societies with high values encourage thrift and efforts in modern education as a way to prepare for the future.	7	35	35	28
Indulgence	the degree to which gratify basic and natural human drives and needs. Societies with high values (indulgence) allow relatively free gratification of the drives related to enjoying life and having fun. Societies with low values (restraint) suppress gratification of needs and regulate it by means of strict social norms.	4	70	55	67

1. the country values are taken from: url here

existence of Egyptian staff, the solution to relational uncertainty was similar to the actions we have discussed above. Personal relationships were built between service engineers and customer employees. Regular meetings to discuss the status and possible problems between local managers as well as irregular meetings between senior managers of the provider and their customer add to this building of interorganisational trust. Relationships are built on all organisational levels.

However, some relational uncertainty remains. A European company typically has a different organisation culture from an Egyptian company – different processes, different hierarchical structures. For example, Egyptian culture has high power distance while Northern Europeans pride themselves on horizontal organisations. Table 10.1 lists the different values researchers have given to different cultural characteristics in Egypt and some selected Northern European countries. This gives an indication of the cultural spread between Northern Europe and Egypt. Having to engage in collaborative relationships that need to last over extended periods of time – service contracts or this type often span 5 to 10 years – such differences are bound to create misunderstandings, problems and even conflicts between the parties. Learning to live and work with other organisations that possess different attitudes, cultures and subsequently make fundamentally different decisions and action is a core part of overcoming the inevitably high level of relational uncertainty in cross-national and cross-cultural business ventures.

ENVIRONMENTAL UNCERTAINTY

The uncertainty for cross-national and cross-cultural business endeavours like the service arrangement between our northern European provider and their Egyptian customer is environmental uncertainty. The provider did not know the local business customers – how to obtain approvals for new installations or technology, how to obtain and negotiate supplies for raw materials and energy or what level of education or skills to expect from new hires. In addition, the Arab Spring caused further disruptions and problems for continued operations.

The service provider solved these very elegantly: much of the environmental uncertainty was regulated in the contract with the customer: the contractual regulation said that these issues were the customer's responsibilities. Organising supply of raw materials was the customer's choice. Getting approvals for installing new equipment and technology was likewise the customer's responsibility. Their motto was 'The one who knows how to do it should do it': a clever solution.

This still left the service provider with the issue of ensuring that qualified staff were available. After all, they wanted a partly Egyptian local organisation without having to change any of the processes and quality standards the company knew from northern Europe. However, what they found was that the education level was not the same: Egyptian engineers did not have the same level of practical experience after graduating from universities as the graduates in northern Europe and generally needed longer to be "settled" professionally in the provider's organisation. In this ramp-up period, the Egyptian engineers would need additional training on the equipment and further IT and language training.

The service provider chose an interesting action to solve this environmental uncertainty. They partnered up with the local university that trained the Egyptian engineers and jointly developed a course that would improve the university's level of education and the availability of trained staff for the provider. This allowed them to find a sustainable way of advancing the industrial need in Egypt. It also helped the provider to reduce the level of additional training every new member of staff they would hire. A win–win situation.

So far, the service provider had been able to deal with anything that the cross-national and cross-cultural service business threw at them. They managed to address the organisational, relational and environmental uncertainty this business brought with it. And then came the Arab Spring. The Arab Spring became known as a wave of political unrests and demonstrations that swept through North Africa and the Middle East: countries such as Tunisia, Libya, Yemen, Iraq, Jordan and also Egypt were affected. The unrests and protests brought much of the political and economic life in these countries to a standstill. The future of people living and operating in these countries – from individuals to organisations – was uncertain.

In Egypt, the government was ousted twice during the Arab Spring. The country experienced two waves of violent protests, the most deadly of which happened in Tahrir Square in the centre of Cairo. Just when things started to look as if they would calm down, the second wave stirred up life in Egypt once more. Figure 10.2 shows the timeline of the major events in Egypt during the Arab Spring.

No one had anticipated the Arab Spring and the extent of the impact it would have on businesses in the area, at least not in the level of severity and the disruption and destruction it brought with it in the end. The supply of resources such as electricity and gas became low. By spring 2011, the lack of resources had led to noticeable disruptions. In heat of 30 and 40 degrees Celsius, people were not allowed to use their air conditioning. Machinery and

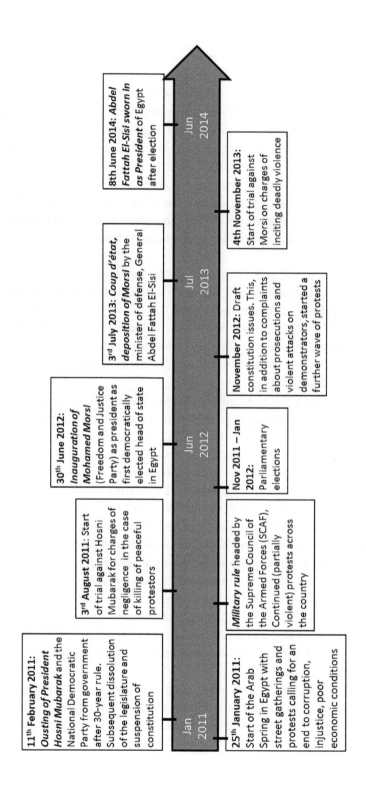

11th February 2011: *Ousting of President Hosni Mubarak* and the National Democratic Party from government after 30-year rule. Subsequent dissolution of the legislature and suspension of constitution

3rd August 2011: Start of trial against Hosni Mubarak for charges of negligence in the case of killing of peaceful protestors

30th June 2012: *Inauguration of Mohamed Morsi* (Freedom and Justice Party) as president as first democratically elected head of state in Egypt

3rd July 2013: *Coup d'état, deposition of Morsi* by the minister of defense, General Abdel Fattah El-Sisi

8th June 2014: *Abdel Fattah El-Sisi sworn in as President* of Egypt after election

Jan 2011

Jun 2012

Jul 2013

Jun 2014

25th January 2011: Start of the Arab Spring in Egypt with street gatherings and protests calling for an end to corruption, injustice, poor economic conditions

Military rule headed by the Supreme Council of the Armed Forces (SCAF), Continued (partially violent) protests across the country

Nov 2011 – Jan 2012: Parliamentary elections

November 2012: Draft constitution issues. This, in addition to complaints about prosecutions and violent attacks on demonstrators, started a further wave of protests

4th November 2013: Start of trial against Morsi on charges of inciting deadly violence

FIGURE 10.2 TIMELINE OF MAJOR EVENTS OF THE ARAB SPRING IN EGYPT

equipment stood idle because there was not enough electricity to keep them running. Staff stayed away from their work places to attend protests, or had to be home between 5 p.m. and 7 a.m because of the curfew.

Our service provider suddenly faced a challenge of an unanticipated and yet very fundamental nature to their business. Staff were not available or when they were, it was difficult to ensure their safety travelling to work. Raw material and process inputs were not available as energy and fuel shortages began to bite. The future was inherently uncertain: no one could predict who the new government would be, what their agenda and policy decisions would be and how long they would stay in power. This was a situation of high uncertainty. It was impossible to predict what would happen a week into the future, let alone a year or even five years.

This situation would provide challenges for any business. Any company would struggle with the difficulties a major event such as the Arab Spring would throw at them, and many businesses did go out of business in Egypt, North Africa and the Middle East. Many international businesses pulled their investments out of the region or were forced to terminate operations. But what could you do if this was not a viable option? What could our service provider do to rectify the situation?

There was not a simple or best answer. The service provider ensured that they responded to events as quickly as possible and stayed observant and receptive of developments during the Arab Spring. They came up with a contingency plan so they could keep their equipment running even during these difficult times, and the contingency plan updated with every new development in Egypt. When the curfew was instigated in 2013, they made sure that staff were still available when and where it they were needed. When the electricity supply was low and the equipment could not run, they ensured that inspections and other service activities were done during this time so that everything would be up and running when the supplies were flowing again.

During this time, they communicated regularly with their customers. They told them as soon as they had a contingency plan. They agreed possible actions and options. They involved the customer every step of the way because they understood that this was a difficult situation for all of them, and their customers appreciated this effort and trusted them with their plan and with dealing with the situation.

Actions based on uncertainty very much mattered for the organisations. It helped them deal with ongoing problems for their businesses and enabled them to keep things going when exceptional circumstances such as the Arab Spring made "business as usual" impossible.

CHAPTER 11

Conclusions

Uncertainty is a central part of our lives. It exists in (almost) every endeavour we have – whether in our private or professional lives. Conversely, it has received much attention by researchers from various fields such as psychology, management, engineering, computer sciences or medicine. Uncertainty is an inherent part of scientific research and some researchers make uncertainty a central part of their work.

My personal research journey began with investigating individuals' perceptions of and reactions to uncertainty. It aimed to answer questions such as how do we act when we face things that we can simply not know? What is it that we do and why? Following this, my research took me into the realm of organisations and how they act and react in the face of uncertainty. What is the difference between individuals and organisations facing uncertainty? Answering these questions has been the core part of my work so far.

This book followed the journey of my research. First, we looked at individuals and uncertainty, then we extended our view on organisations and uncertainty. We have been able to make some interesting connections, identify some curious similarities and unexpected differences.

Uncertainty is an undeniable part of our lives and we have seen that research has a considerable amount to catch up in that regard. In his book *The Monk and the Riddle*, where Randy Komisar recalled his experience of leaving the predefined path of his career and creating a job for himself as virtual CEO, he says "Change is certain, and in a world of constant change, we actually control very little". This means we need to be able to cope and thrive in the face of uncertainty.

Uncertainty and Uncertainty Perception

The scientific investigations into uncertainty are relatively recent. Psychology told us in the 1970s that we do not act following rational rules when facing uncertainty. Since then, many experiments and other scientific endeavours have confirmed this statement and have tried to tell us why this is the case.

Why do we feel fear in the face of uncertainty? Why do we often downplay the impact that uncertainty has in our lives? How do we typically respond to uncertainty? These are the issues that many researchers have investigated in different areas of life. These are also some of the questions we investigated in this book.

Organisations also face uncertainty, and for them ignoring it or making an unsuitable response to uncertainty may well lead to a disastrous end. The stakes are higher and much more urgent. In this book, we looked at some of the similarities between the behaviours of individuals and organisations to show what lessons they can learn from each other.

Uncertainty exists as an own concept, as extant uncertainty. Our future is uncertain and some scenarios are more likely to occur than others. Restaurants we dine in may have food of varying quality and there may be a certain level of likelihood that we receive an outstandingly good (or bad) dish. The weather of tomorrow or next week cannot be predicted with absolute certainty. Similarly, organisations face extant uncertainty. Their environments have a certain level of turbulence and dynamism that makes them more or less predictable. Their collaboration partners are always able to act opportunistically.

This may be easier to express in some situations than in others. We usually agree on probabilities such as getting a certain number when throwing dice or when tossing a coin. The extant uncertainty in these examples is one in six and one in two respectively. In other situations, we can merely guess or have approximate measures of extant uncertainty. With tools such as Monte Carlo modelling, we try to mimic many possible future scenarios until we have a probability-like distribution. We help ourselves to try and identify the true levels of extant uncertainty.

Then there is also our perception of this uncertainty, which may or may not match the extant uncertainty. We showed that in most cases, our perception does not match extant uncertainty. We tend to be overconfident and underestimate uncertainty. People may invent a higher rationale for observations they make under uncertainty. These higher rationales can be to blame their "skills" when they are repeatedly being right or wrong. This phenomenon also holds when people know better. In other words, it is an automatic reaction to situations that are influenced by uncertainty.

Organisations do the same thing – they observe and perceive their environment, their partners and themselves. Yet research is thus far very limited in this aspect and does not share the same wealth of insights for organisations as it does for individuals. No research has compared organisations' perceptions of uncertainty to the extant uncertainty they face. The truth is that we do not even know how to measure extant uncertainty of organisations, let alone their perception of this uncertainty. Organisations and their environments are too complex and complicated to apply simple measures. All approximations and simplifications included in measurements do not tell the whole story.

Thus there is still much work to be done in this field – to increase our insights both into individual and organisational perception of uncertainty. The work researchers have done so far has understood uncertainty mainly as a negative concept that induces fear, makes us indecisive and reduces our ability to reach our true potential. Similarly for organisations, uncertainty is an essential part of their everyday operations but it essentially limits organisations' ability to be "truly" innovative and ground-breaking. It moderates organisational activity. At least this seems to be the underlying assumption of most current research. Thus much work remains to be done.

Uncertainty and Decision Making

Most of our decisions are made under uncertainty, whether in our private or professional lives. This poses a difficulty for us, because we do not have all the information we need to make an optimal or even a good decision. There is always room for missed opportunities and regret.

We discussed that we come to our decisions in two different ways using the two systems of reasoning. System 1 is impulsive and fast and gives us our immediate emotional responses to a situation. System 2 is rule-based and slow and gives us a calculated answer taking into the account the information that is available. When both systems come to the same conclusions, we are ready to make a decision. Our gut and our brain tell us the same thing. Problems arise when this is not the case and our gut tells us a different story than our brain. In practice this may not be the case too often, but when it does happen it can cause us to go for the wrong option, leaving room for regret and disappointment in the long run.

Decision-making biases are an example of when Systems 1 and 2 tell us something different. Our gut would choose option 1 while our brain would choose option 2. If asked about the length of the river Elbe and we had just talked about the book *20,000 Leagues Under the Sea*, we would in all likelihood give a higher number than if we had just thought about the current price of butter. Similarly, when we leave the motorway and come into a town or city where we need to drive at 50 km/h, we will experience this speed as very slow. System 1 is responsible for anchoring our evaluations, and thus it determines which information we consider.

Decision-making biases mean that predictions by decision theory are typically not observed in the real world. Predictions of decision theory are basically the values that our System 2 would give if it was not reined in by System 1. But we saw also that our System 1 is important and often even essential for us when making decisions. We are in the need of both of them.

In managerial decision making, we still have a very limited understanding of uncertainty and its impact on the decision maker, the decision-making process and the appropriate managerial actions. It can even be challenging to have a focused discussion about uncertainty and its role in organisational processes with managers in practice. Often the implicit understanding of what uncertainty is (and is not) is difficult to articulate.

Yet uncertainty is part of (almost) every organisational decision-making process. Most managers consider it through a mix of experience-based and model-based approaches, although the role of each can differ quite significantly depending on the type of decision problem they face. In situations of high uncertainty, decision makers seem to yearn for some form of decision support through models and predictions. This may be counterintuitive but it highlights the applicability of many of the findings from psychology research in organisational settings. Uncertainty is a fundamental concept in our daily and professional lives and understanding the impact it has is essential, especially in an organisational context.

Our understanding of uncertainty is limited and leaves room for much further work. To what degree are insights in individual's decision making under uncertainty applicable to organisations? What decision biases are of importance and when do they apply? How can the impact of these biases be overcome? How do these perceptions influence decision outcome and business success? How does uncertainty need to be communicated to support decision making? These and many more questions are still unresolved and much more research work is needed to explore this field and answer these and further questions.

Uncertainty and Actions

Uncertainty is the starting point of many of our actions. When we are uncertain, we may feel the need to reduce this uncertainty by collecting new information and increasing our knowledge. This seems a logical first reaction. You don't know something you have a need to know – go out and find what you are missing. Naturally, this is also what theory has told us to do. Uncertainty presents an obstacle to us so we should attempt to reduce it. But there is so much more to possible actions to be taken under uncertainty.

Many individual and organisational adventures are only possible when we embrace uncertainty and use it to our advantage. New creations such as writing a book or making new friends do by definition venture into the unknown. So do innovations in organisations: developing new products or services, reinventing the organisation philosophy or entering new markets. These actions require us to overcome our initial fear of uncertainty and invite ourselves into the process. We have to solve the questions that arise one step at a time rather than wait until we have all the answers before deciding which path to go down.

Yet this second view on uncertainty is underexplored in academic works. Uncertainty is rarely if not ever seen in its potential for new ventures, whether on an individual or organisational level. It is rarely conceptualised as the enabler of new activities, of innovation, creativity and sustained success. It is usually portrayed as the reason for disruptions; it mitigates individual and organisational decision-making and the feeling of security in action taking. The view of uncertainty as the root cause for possibilities has been largely ignored in the different scientific fields that investigate uncertainty. And yet there is so much to be done in this area.

So much to do and so little time.

References

Chapter 1 Introduction

Courtney, H., 2001. *20/20 Foresight: Crafting Strategy in an Uncertain World.* Harvard Business School Press, Boston, Massachussetts, USA

Courtney, H., Kirkland, J. and Viguerie, P., 1997. Strategy Under Uncertainty. *Harvard Business Review,* 75(6), pp. 67–79.

Grishin, S., 2009. Uncertainty as a Creative Force in Visual Art. In G. Bammer and M. Smithson, eds. *Uncertainty and Risk: Multidisciplinary Perspectives.* London: Earthscan, pp. 115–125.

Ionita, M., 2009, Variability and potential predictability of Elbe river streamflow and their relationship to global teleconnection patterns. PhD Thesis, University of Bremen

Kahneman, D. and Tversky, A., 1982. Variants of Uncertainty. *Cognition,* 11(2), pp. 143–157.

Koźmiński, A., 2015. Management in the Time of "Generalized Uncertainty": the Question of Relevance. Plenary Session at EurAM (European Academy of Management Conference), 19 June 2015, Warsaw, Poland.

Mackey, J., 2009. Musical Improvisation, Creativity and Uncertainty. In G. Bammer and M. Smithson, eds. *Uncertainty and Risk: Multidisciplinary Perspectives.* London: Earthscan, pp. 105–113.

Soanes, C., 2005. *The Oxford English Dictionary.* Oxford: Oxford University Press.

Chapter 2 Perceiving Uncertainty

Alpert, M. and Raiffa, H., 1982. A Progress Report on the Training of Probability Assessors. In D. Kahneman, P. Slovic, and A. Tversky, eds. *Judgement under Uncertainty: Heuristics and Biases*. Harvard University: Cambridge University Press, pp. 294–305.

Brown, T.A., 1973. *An Experiment on Probabilistic Forecasting*. Santa Monica, CA: The RAND Corp.

Dawes, R.M., 1988. *Rational Choice in an Uncertain World*. San Diego, CA: Harcourt Brace Jovanovich Publishers.

Elouedi, Z., Mellouli, K. and Smets, P., 2001. Belief Decision Trees: Theoretical Foundations. *International Journal of Approximate Reasoning*, 28(2–3), pp. 91–124.

Giordani, P. and Söderlind, P., 2003. Inflation Forecast Uncertainty. *European Economic Review*, 47(6), pp. 1037–1059.

Harvey, N., 2001. Improving Judgement in Forecasting. In J. S. Armstrong, ed. *Principles of Forecasting: A Handbook for Researchers and Practitioners*. New York, NY: Springer Science and Business Media, pp. 59–80.

Kahneman, D., Slovic, P. and Tversky, A., 1982. *Judgment Under Uncertainty: Heuristics and Biases*. Cambridge, UK: Cambridge University Press.

Kreye, M.E., Goh, Y.M., Newnes, L.B. and Goodwin, P., 2012. Approaches of Displaying Information to Assist Decisions under Uncertainty. *Omega – International Journal of Management Science*, 40(6), pp. 682–692.

Langer, E.J., 1975. The Illusion of Control. *Journal of Personality and Social Psychology*, 32(2), pp. 311–328.

Langer, E.J. and Roth, J., 1975. Heads I Win, Tails is Chance: The Illusion of Control is a Function of the Sequence of Outcomes in a Purely Chance Task. *Journal of Personality and Social Psychology*, 32(1975), pp. 951–955.

Lichtenstein, S. and Fischhoff, B., 1977. Do those who know more also know more about how much they know? *Organizational Behavior and Human Performance*, 20(2), pp. 159–183.

Lichtenstein, S. and Fischhoff, B., 1980. Training for Calibration. *Organizational Behavior and Human Performance*, 26(1980), pp. 149–171.

Lichtenstein, S., Fischhoff, B. and Phillips, L.D., 1982. Calibration of Probabilities: The State of the Art to 1980. In D. Kahnemann, P. Slovic, and A. Tversky, eds. *Judgement under Uncertainty: Heuristics and Biases*. Cambridge, UK: Cambridge University Press, pp. 306–334.

Morgan, M.G. and Henrion, M., 1990. *Uncertainty – A Guide to Dealing with Uncertainty in Quantitative Risk and Policy Analysis*. Cambridge, UK: Cambridge University Press.

O'Connor, M. and Lawrence, M., 1989. An Examination of the Accuracy of Judgmental Confidence Intervals in Time Series Forecasting. *Journal of Forecasting*, 8(1989), pp. 141–155.

Phadke, M.S., 1989. *Quality Engineering Using Robust Design*. Englewood Cliffs, NJ: Prentice Hall.

Pickhardt, R.C. and Wallace, J.B.A., 1974. A Study of the Performance of Subjective Probability Assessors. *Decision Science*, 5(1974), pp. 347–363.

Pitz, G.F., 1974. Subjective Probability Distributions for Imperfectly Known Quantities. In L.W. Gregg, ed. *Knowledge and cognition*. Oxford: Lawrence Erlbaum, pp. 29–42.

Selvidge, J., 1980. Assessing the Extremes of Probability Distributions by the Fractile Method. *Decision Science*, 11(1980), pp. 493–502.

Chapter 3 Expressing Uncertainty

Brun, W. and Teigen, K.H., 1988. Verbal Probabilities: Ambiguous, Context-dependent, or Both? *Organizational Behavior and Human Decision Processes*, 41(3), pp. 390–404.

Capriotti, K. and Waldrup, B.E., 2005. Miscommunication Of Uncertainties in Financial Statements: A Study of Preparers and Users. *Journal of Business and Economics Research*, 3(1), pp. 33–46.

Du, N. and Stevens, K., 2011. Numeric-to-verbal Translation of Probability Expressions in SFAS 5. *Managerial Auditing Journal*, 26(3), pp. 248–262.

Helton, J.C., 1997. Uncertainty and Sensitivity Analysis in the Presence of Stochastic and Subjective Uncertainty. *Journal of Statistical Computation and Simulation*, 57(1–4), pp. 3–76.

Nelson, T.O. and Narens, L., 1980. Norms of 300 General-information Questions: Accuracy of Recall, Latency of Recall, and Feeling-of-knowing Ratings. *Journal of Verbal Learning and Verbal Behavior*, 19(3), pp. 338–368.

Renooij, S. and Witteman, C., 1999. Talking Probabilities: Communicating Probabilistic Information with Words and Numbers. *International Journal of Approximate Reasoning*, 22(3), pp. 169–194.

Smith, V. and Clark, H., 1993. On the Course of Answering Questions. *Journal of Memory and Language*, 32(1), pp. 25–38.

Stone, D.R. and Johnson, R.J., 1959. A Study of Words Indicating Frequency. *Journal of Educational Psychology*, 50(5), 224–227.

Szarvas, G., Vincze, V. Farkas, R., Móra, G. and Gurevych, I., 2012. Cross-genre and Cross-domain Detection of Semantic Uncertainty. *Computational Linguistics*, 38(2), pp. 335–367.

Tabandeh, A.S., 1994. Characterising Artificial Intelligence Technology for International Transfer. *AI and Society*, 8(4), pp. 315–325.

Teigen, K.H. and Brun, W., 1995. Yes, But it is Uncertain: Direction and Communicative Intention of Verbal Probabilistic Terms. *Acta Psychologica*, 88(3), pp. 233–258.

Van der Gaag, L.C., Renooij, S., Witteman, C.L.M., Aleman, B.M.P. and Taal, B.G., 1999. *How to Elicit Many Probabilities*. Utrecht: Utrecht University.

Van der Sluijs, J.P., Craye, M., Funtowicz, S., Kloprogge, P., Ravetz, J. and Risbey, J., 2005. Combining Quantitative and Qualitative Measures of Uncertainty in Model-based Environmental Assessment: The NUSAP System. *Risk Analysis: An International Journal*, 25(2), pp. 481–492.

Wallsten, T.S., Budescu, D.V. and Zwick, R., 1993. Comparing the Calibration and Coherence of Numerical and Verbal Probability Judgments. *Management Science*, 39(2), pp. 176–190.

Windschitl, P.D. and Wells, G.L., 1996. Measuring Psychological Uncertainty: Verbal Versus Numeric Methods. *Journal of Experimental Psychology: Applied*, 2(4), pp. 343–364.

Zimmermann, H.-J., 2000. An Application-oriented View of Modeling Uncertainty. *European Journal of Operational Research*, 122(2000), pp. 190–198.

Chapter 4 Accepting Uncertainty

Ashford, S.J., 1986. Feedback-seeking Behavior in Individual Adaptation: A Resource Perspective. *Academy of Management Journal*, 29(3), 465–487.

Ashford, S.J. and Cummings, L.L., 1983. Feedback as an Individual Resource: Personal Strategies of Creating Information. *Organizational Behavior and Human Performance*, 32(3), 370–398.

Bammer, G. and Smithson, M., 2009. *Uncertainty and Risk: Multidisciplinary Perspectives*. London: Earthscan.

Berger, C.R., 1979. Beyond Initial Interaction: Uncertainty, Understanding, and the Development of Interpersonal Relationships. *Language and Social Psychology*, pp. 122–144.

Berger, C.R. and Calabrese, R.J., 1975. Some Explorations in Initial Interaction and Beyond: Toward a Developmental Theory of Interpersonal Communication. *Human Communication Research*, 1(2), 99–112.

Cameron, K.S., Kim, M.U. and Whetten, D.A., 1987. Organizational Effects of Decline and Turbulence. *Administrative Science Quarterly*, 32(2), pp. 222–240.

Cialdini, R.B., 2007. *Influence: The Psychology of Persuasion*, 3rd edn. New York, NY: Harper Collins Publishers.

De Bruin, W.B. et al., 2002. What Number is "Fifty–Fifty"?: Redistributing Excessive 50% Responses in Elicited Probabilities. *Risk Analysis: An International Journal*, 22(4), pp. 713–723.

Gambetta, D., 1988. Can we Trust Trust? In D. Gambetta, ed. *Trust: Making and Breaking Cooperative Relations*. Oxford: Basil Blackwell Ltd, pp. 213–238.

Gulati, R., 1995. Does Familiarity Breed Trust? The Implications of Repeated Ties for Contractual Choice in Alliances. *The Academy of Management Journal*, 38(1), pp. 85–112.

Ji, L., Peng, K. and Nisbett, R., 2000. Culture, Control, and Perception of Relationships in the Environment. *Journal of Personality and Social Psychology.* 78(5), pp. 943–955.

Kahneman, D. and Tversky, A., 1979. Prospect Theory: An Analysis of Decision under Risk. *Econometrica*, 47(2), pp. 263–291.

Loewenstein, G.F., Weber, E.U., Hsee, C.K. and Welch, N., 2001. Risk as Feelings. *Psychological Bulletin*, 127(2), pp. 267–286.

Rokeach, M., 1960. *The Open and Closed Minds*. New York, NY: Basic Books.

Smith, C. and Ellsworth, P., 1985. Patterns of Cognitive Appraisal in Emotion. *Journal of Personality and Social Psychology*, 48(4), pp. 813–838.

Chapter 5 Deciding Under Uncertainty

Arkes, H.R., 1991. Costs and Benefits of Judgment Errors: Implications for Debiasing. *Psychological Bulletin*, 110(3), pp. 486–498.

BBC, 2012. L'Aquila Quake: Italy Scientists Guilty of Manslaughter. Available at: http://www.bbc.com/news/world-europe-20025626.

BBC, 2014. L'Aquila Quake: Scientists see Convictions Overturned. Available at: http://www.bbc.com/news/world-europe-29996872.

BBC, 2015. US Snow: National Weather Service Admits Forecast Error. Available at: http://www.bbc.com/news/world-us-canada-30996010.

Berger, C.R. and Calabrese, R.J., 1975. Some Explorations in Initial Interaction and Beyond: Toward a Developmental Theory of Interpersonal Communication. *Human Communication Research*, 1(2), pp. 99–112.

Chapman, G. and Johnson, E., 1999. Anchoring, Activation, and the Construction of Values. *Organizational Behavior and Human Decision Processes*, 79(2), pp. 115–153.

Elouedi, Z., Mellouli, K. and Smets, P., 2001. Belief Decision Trees: Theoretical Foundations. *International Journal of Approximate Reasoning*, 28(2–3), pp. 91–124.

Evans, J.S.B.T. and Over, D.E., 1996. *Rationality and Reasoning*. Hove, UK: Psychology Press.

Fischhoff, B., 2003. Hindsight ≠ Foresight: the Effect of Outcome Knowledge on Judgment Under Uncertainty. *Quality and Safety in Health Care*, 12(2003), pp. 304–311.

Gudykunst, W.B. and Nishida, T., 2001. Anxiety, Uncertainty, and Perceived Effectiveness of Communication Across Relationships and Cultures. *International Journal of Intercultural Relations*, 25(1), pp. 55–71.

Howell, J.L. and Shepperd, J.A., 2012. Reducing Information Avoidance Through Affirmation. *Psychological Science*, 23(2), pp. 141–145.

Kahneman, D., 2011. *Thinking, Fast and Slow*. New York, NY: Farrar, Strauss and Giroux.

Kahneman, D., Slovic, P. and Tversky, A., 1982. *Judgment Under Uncertainty: Heuristics and Biases.* Cambridge, UK: Cambridge University Press.

LeBoeuf, R.A. and Shafir, E., 2006. The Long and Short of it: Physical Anchoring Effects. *Journal of Behavioral Decision Making,* 19(4), pp. 393–406.

Levin, I.P., Schnittjer, S.K. and Thee, S.L., 1988. Information Framing Effects in Social and Personal Decisions. *Journal of Experimental Social Psychology,* 24(6), pp. 520–529.

Loewenstein, G.F., Weber, E.U., Hsee, C.K. and Welch, N., 2001. Risk as Feelings. *Psychological Bulletin,* 127(2), pp. 267–286.

Morgan, M.G. and Henrion, M., 1990. *Uncertainty – A Guide to Dealing with Uncertainty in Quantitative Risk and Policy Analysis.* Cambridge, UK: Cambridge University Press.

Nisbett, R.E., Peng, K., Choi, I. and Norenzayan, A, 2001. Culture and Systems of Thought: Holistic Versus Analytic Cognition. *Psychological Review,* 108(2), pp. 291–310.

Osman, M., 2004. An Evaluation of Dual-process Theories of Reasoning. *Psychonomic Bulletin and Review,* 11(6), pp. 988–1010.

Sears, D.O. and Freedman, J.L., 1967. Selective Exposure to Information: A Critical Review. *The Public Opinion Quarterly,* 31(2), pp. 194–213.

Sloman, S.A., 1996. The Empirical Case for Two Systems of Reasoning. *Psychological Bulletin,* 119(1), pp. 3–22.

——, 2002. Two Systems of Reasoning. In T. Gilovich, D. Griffin, and D. Kahneman, eds. *Heuristics and Biases: The Psychology of Intuitive Judgment.* New York, NY: Cambridge University Press, pp. 379–396.

Smithson, M., 2009. Psychology's Ambivalent View of Uncertainty. In G. Bammer and M. Smithson, eds. *Uncertainty and Risk – Multidisciplinary Perspectives.* London: Earthscan, pp. 205–218.

Wilson, T.D. and Schooler, J.W. 1991. Thinking Too Much: Introspection Can Reduce the Quality of Preferences and Decisions. *Journal of Personality and Social Psychology*, 60(2), pp. 181–192.

Windschitl, P.D. and Wells, G.L., 1996. Measuring Psychological Uncertainty: Verbal Versus Numeric Methods. *Journal of Experimental Psychology: Applied*, 2(4), pp. 343–364.

Chapter 6 Acting on Uncertainty

Bammer, G. and Smithson, M., 2009. *Uncertainty and Risk: Multidisciplinary Perspectives*. London: Earthscan.

Blandin, J.S. and Brown, W.B., 1977. Uncertainty and Management's Search for Information. *IEEE Transactions on Engineering Management*, 24(4), pp. 114–119.

Berchicci, L. and Tucci, C.L., 2010. There is More to Market Learning than Gathering Good Information: The Role of Shared Team Values in Radical Product Definition. *Journal of Product Innovation Management*, 27(7), pp. 972–990.

Campos Silva, D.D., Santiago, L.P. and Silva, P.M.S., 2012. Impact of Premature Information Transfer on Cost and Development Time of Projects. *IEEE Transactions on Engineering Management*, (99), pp. 1–13.

Daft, R.L. and Lengel, R.H., 1983. Information Richness: A New Approach to Managerial Behavior and Organization Design. In B. Staw and L.L. Cummings, eds. *Research in Organizational Behavior*. Connecticut: JAI Press.

Daft, R.L. and Lengel, R.H., 1986. Organizational Information Requirements, Media Richness and Structural Design. *Management Science*, 32(5), pp. 554–571.

Fidel, R. and Green, M., 2004. The Many Faces of Accessibility: Engineers' Perception of Information Sources. *Information Processing and Management*, 40(3), pp. 563–581.

Fields, J., 2011. *Uncertainty: Turning Fear and Doubt into Fuel for Brilliance.* New York, NY: Penguin Books.

Fischhoff, B., Slovic, P., Lichtenstein, S., Read, S. and Combs, B., 1978. How Safe is Safe Enough? A Psychometric Study of Attitudes Towards Technological Risks and Benefits. *Policy Sciences*, 9(2), pp. 127–152.

Fu, K., Cagan, J. and Kotovsky, K., 2010. Design Team Convergence: The Influence of Example Solution Quality. *Journal of Mechanical Design*, 132, pp. 1–11.

Grishin, S., 2009. Uncertainty as a Creative Force in Visual Art. In G. Bammer and M. Smithson, eds. *Uncertainty and Risk: Multidisciplinary Perspectives.* London: Earthscan, pp. 115–125.

Johnson, E.J., Hershey, J., Meszaros, J. and Kunreuther, H., 1993. Framing, Probability Distortions, and Insurance Decisions. *Journal of Risk and Uncertainty*, 7, pp. 35–51.

Kwasitsu, L., 2004. Information-seeking Behavior of Design, Process, and Manufacturing Engineers. *Library and Information Science Research*, 25(4), pp. 459–476.

Lynn, G.S., Reilly, R.R. and Akgun, A.E., 2000. Knowledge Management in New Product Teams: Practices and Outcomes. *IEEE Transactions on Engineering Management*, 47(2), pp. 221–231.

Miles, A., Voorwinden, S., Chapman, S. and Wardle, J., 2008. Psychologic Predictors of Cancer Information Avoidance among Older Adults: The Role of Cancer Fear and Fatalism. *Cancer Epidemiology Biomarkers and Prevention*, 17(8), pp. 1872–1879.

Patanakul, P., Chen, J. and Lynn, G.S., 2012. Autonomous Teams and New Product Development. *Journal of Product Innovation Management*, 29(5), pp. 734–750.

Robinson, M.A., 2010. An Empirical Analysis of Engineers' Information Behaviors. *Journal of the American Society for Information Science and Technology*, 61(4), pp. 640–658.

Slater, S.F. and Narver, J.C., 1995. Market Orientation and the Learning Organization. *Journal of Marketing*, 59(3), pp. 63–74.

Song, M., Van Der Bij, H. and Weggeman, M., 2005. Determinants of the Level of Knowledge Application: A Knowledge-based and Information-processing Perspective. *Journal of Product Innovation Management*, 22(5), pp. 430–444.

Van Riel, A.C.R., Lemmink, J. and Ouwersloot, H., 2004. High-technology Service Innovation Success: A Decision-making Perspective. *Journal of Product Innovation Management*, 21(5), pp. 348–359.

Varis, M. and Littunen, H., 2010. Types of Innovation, Sources of Information and Performance in Entrepreneurial SMEs. *European Journal of Innovation Management*, 13(2), pp. 128–154.

Wallerstein, I., 1997. Uncertainty and Creativity. Talk at Forum 2000: Concerns and Hopes on the Threshold of the New Millennium in Prague, Czech Republic, Sept. 3–6.

Yates, J.F., Lee, J.-W. and Shinotsuka, H., 1996. Beliefs about Overconfidence, Including its Cross-national Variation. *Organizational Behavior and Human Decision Processes*, 65(2), pp. 138–147.

Chapter 7 Organisations and Uncertainty Types

Brashers, D.E., 2001. Communication and Uncertainty Management. *Journal of Communication*, 51(3), pp. 477–497.

Chow, C.C. and Sarin, R.K., 2002. Known, Unknown, and Unknowable Uncertainties. *Theory and Decision*, 52(2), pp. 127–138.

De Meyer, A., Loch, C.H. and Pich, M.T., 2002. Managing Project Uncertainty: From Variation to Chaos. *MIT Sloan Management Review*, 43(2), pp. 60–67.

Friedman, T.L., 2005. *The World is Flat – The Globalized World in the Twenty-first Century*. New York, NY: Penguin Group.

Kreye, M.E., Newnes, L.B. and Goh, Y.M., 2014. Uncertainty in Competitive Bidding – A Framework for Product-service Systems. *Production Planning and Control*, 25(6), pp. 462–477.

Pfeffer, J. and Salancik, G.R., 1978. *The External Control of Organizations: A Resource Dependence Perspective*. Stanford, CA: Stanford University Press.

Chapter 8 Uncertainty and Time

Bedford, T. and Cooke, R., 2001. What is uncertainty? In T. Bedford and R. Cooke, ed. *Probabilistic Risk Analysis: Foundations and Methods*, pp. 17–38. Cambridge University Press, Cambridge, UK.

Board, D., 2010. Leadership: The Ghost at the Trillion Dollar Crash? *European Management Journal*, 28(4), pp. 269–277.

Brand, S., 1999. *The Clock of the Long Now: Time and Responsibility*. London: Weidenfeld and Nicolson.

Courtney, H., 2001. *20/20 Foresight: Crafting Strategy in an Uncertain World*. Harvard Business School Press.

Gareis, R., 2010. Changes of Organizations by Projects. *International Journal of Project Management*, 28(4), pp. 314–327.

Geraldi, J. G., Lee-Kelley, L., and Kutsch, E., 2010. The Titanic sunk, so what? Project manager response to unexpected events. *International Journal of Project Management*, 28 (6), 547–558.

Kotter, J.P., 1995. Leading Change: Why Transformation Efforts Fail. *Harvard Business Review*, 73(2).

Petit, Y. and Hobbs, B., 2010. Project Portfolios in Dynamic Environments: Sources of Uncertainty and Sensing Mechanisms. *Project Management Journal*, 41(4), pp. 46–58.

Sommer, S.C. and Loch, C.H., 2009. Incentive Contracts in Projects with Unforeseeable Uncertainty. *Production and Operations Management*, 18(2), pp. 185–196.

Chapter 9 Uncertainty and Organisational Decision Making

Bourgeois, L.J., McAllister, D.W. and Mitchell, T.R., 1978. The Effects of Different Organizational Environments upon Decisions about Organizational Structure. *Academy of Management Journal*, 21, pp. 508–514.

Cameron, K.S., Kim, M.U. and Whetten, D.A., 1987. Organizational Effects of Decline and Turbulence. *Administrative Science Quarterly*, 32(2), pp. 222–240.

Carmeli, A. and Schaubroeck, J., 2008. Organisational Crisis-preparedness: The Importance of Learning from Failures. *Long Range Planning*, 41(2), pp. 177–196.

Christianson, M.K., Farkas, M.T., Sutcliffe, K.M., Weick, K.E., 2009. Learning Through Rare Events: Significant Interruptions at the Baltimore and Ohio Railroad Museum. *Organization Science*, 20(5), pp. 846–860.

Eastburn, R.W. and Boland Jr., R.J., 2015. Inside Banks' Information and Control Systems: Post-decision Surprise and Corporate Disruption. *Information and Organization*, 25(3), pp. 160–190.

European Commission, 2009. *Economic Crisis in Europe: Causes, Consequences and Responses*. Economic and Financial Affairs Series, European Communities, doi: 10.2765/84540, available at: http://ec.europa.eu/economy_finance/publications/publication15887_en.pdf

Knight, J.G., Mitchell, B.S. and Gao, H., 2009. Riding out the Muhammad Cartoons Crisis: Contrasting Strategies and Outcomes. *Long Range Planning*, 42(1), pp. 6–22.

Kreye, M.E., Newnes, L.B. and Goh, Y.M., 2013. Information Availability at the Competitive Bidding Stage for Service. *Journal of Manufacturing Technology Management*, 24(7), pp. 976–997.

Meissner, P. and Wulf, T., 2014. Antecendents and Effects of Decision Comprehensiveness: The Role of Decision Quality and Perceived Uncertainty. *European Management Journal*, 32(4), pp. 625–635.

Mitroff, I.I. and Alpaslan, M.C., 2003. Preparing for Evil. *Harvard Business Review*, 81(4), pp. 109–115.

Pearson, C.M. and Clair, J.A., 1998. Reframing Crisis Management. *The Academy of Management Review*, 23(1), pp. 59–76.

Turner, B.A., 1976. The Organizational and Interorganizational Development of Disasters. *Administrative Science Quarterly*, 21(3), pp. 378–397.

Wilensky, H.L., 1967. *Organizational Intelligence*. New York: Basic Books.

Chapter 10 Taking Action in Organisations

Acquaah, M., 2007. Managerial Social Capital, Strategic Orientation, and Organizational Performance in an Emerging Economy. *Strategic Management Journal*, 28(12), pp. 1235–1255.

Arnold, D.J. and Quelch, J.A., 1998. New Strategies in Emerging Markets. *Sloan Management Review*, 40(1), pp. 7–20.

Bishara, N.D., 2011. Governance and Corruption Constraints in the Middle East: Overcoming the Business Ethics Glass Ceiling. *American Business Law Journal*, 48(2), pp. 227–283.

Cameron, K.S., Kim, M.U. and Whetten, D.A., 1987. Organizational Effects of Decline and Turbulence. *Administrative Science Quarterly*, 32(2), pp. 222–240.

Daft, R.L., Lengel, R.H. and Trevino, L.K., 1987. Message Equivocality, Media Selection, and Manager Performance: Implications for Information Systems. *MIS Quarterly*, 11(3), pp. 355–366.

Hitt, M.A. Ahlstrom, D., Dacin, M.T., Levitas, E., Svobodina, L., 2004. The Institutional Effects on Strategic Alliance Partner Selection in Transition Economies: China vs. Russia. *Organization Science*, 15(2), pp. 173–185.

Hofstede, G. H., 2003. *Cultures consequences: Comparing values, behaviors, institutions and organizations across nations*. 2nd ed. Thousand Oaks, CA, USA: Sage Publications.

Huntington, S.P., 1992. If not Civilizations, what-paradigms of the Post-cold war World. *Foreign Affairs*, 72, p. 186.

Huntington, S.P., 2002, originally published in 1997. *The Clash of Civilizations and the Remaking of World Order*. London: Free Press.

Javidan, M., Dorfman, P.W., De Luque, M.S., House, R.J., 2006. In the Eye of the Beholder: Cross-cultural Lessons in Leadership from Project GLOBE. *Academy of Management Perspectives*, 20(1), pp. 67–90.

Michel, A. and Wortham, S., 2009. *Bullish on Uncertainty: How Organizational Cultures Transform Participants*. New York, NY: Cambridge University Press.

Turner, B.A., 1976. The Organizational and Interorganizational Development of Disasters. *Administrative Science Quarterly*, 21(3), pp. 378–397.

Chapter 11 Conclusions

Komisar, R. and Lineback, K., 2001. *The Monk and the Riddle: The Art of Creating a Life While Making a Living*. Harvard Business School Press, Boston, Massachussetts, USA.

Index

For Product Safety Concerns and Information please contact our EU
representative GPSR@taylorandfrancis.com
Taylor & Francis Verlag GmbH, Kaufingerstraße 24, 80331 München, Germany

www.ingramcontent.com/pod-product-compliance
Ingram Content Group UK Ltd.
Pitfield, Milton Keynes, MK11 3LW, UK
UKHW020947180425
457613UK00019B/571

9 780367 669713